Ant

Ant

Charlotte Sleigh

REAKTION BOOKS

For Mary, who is pretty wise for a two-legged animal.

Published by
REAKTION BOOKS LTD
79 Farringdon Road
London EC1M 3JU, UK
www.reaktionbooks.co.uk

First published 2003

Printed in China

British Library Cataloguing in Publication Data

Sleigh, Charlotte
    Ant. – (Animal)
    1. Ants 2. Animals and civilization
    I. Title
    595.7'96

    ISBN 1 86189 190 3

Contents

Ants (*Formicae*) on an anthill, a miniature from a French bestiary of *c.* 1450.

1 Introduction

It is extraordinarily difficult to avoid using grandiose adjectives in the description of ants.

Ants command a respect from their fans out of all proportion to the insects' size. Ants, they affirm, are the '-est' insects: the cleverest, most organized, hardest-working, most numerous, most fecund, most dominant; they are older than humans, more bellicose, more cooperative, more communicative. Frequently these comparisons border on the bizarre. A children's web site asserts: 'Ant brains are largest amongst insects . . . It has been estimated that an ant's brain may have the same processing power as a Macintosh II computer.'[1]

At least, all this is what myrmecologists (those who study ants) would have us believe. Though their precise claims have changed over time, western students of ants always seem to have made hyperbolic assertions about them.

The eighteenth century natural philosopher Réaumur started at a basic level in his catalogue of the extraordinary qualities of ants: 'we have for them none of those aversions that are frequently entertained towards so many other insects'.[2] Our dispassionate attitude towards them compared to, say, cockroaches, signals their human status; their existence is parallel with our own. Unlike fleas, they have no particular dependence upon us, and we have no need for them as we do for bees.

This independent existence of ants has, at various times, been a source both of wonder and of horror. Thomas Mouffet, a sixteenth-century physician, noted that the ants

> . . . are so exemplary . . . it is no wonder that Plato, Phaedone, hath determined that they who without the help of philosophy have lead a civill life by custom or from their own diligence, they had their souls from Ants, and when they die they are turned to ants again.[3]

Here, the ants' lack of reliance upon philosophy marks out the alternative yet equivalent nature of their civic lives: a parallel so wondrous that, according to Pliny, they are the only creatures besides us that bury their dead with funeral rites. More contemporary analogue-myths assert with equal confidence that ants, if magnified to the size of sheep, would rule the earth, and that in the event of a nuclear holocaust they would outlast humans.

In between the eras of Plato and NATO, observers have concocted a canon of astounding facts and figures concerning the numbers of ants, their distribution, their reproduction and modes of life. They are habitually scaled up to 'equate' to human terms, upon which basis their nests are compared to the pyramids, or to the Great Wall of China, and their movement with that of a speeding train. They have recently been enumerated at ten thousand trillion; collectively they are asserted to weigh as much as the earth's human population. E. O. Wilson, the most renowned living myrmecologist, claims that the behaviour of ants is scientifically more interesting than that of humans' bestial cousin and the psychologists' current favourite, the chimp. The reason for this, he writes, is that ants can be studied for the meaning of their social interaction, whereas the most impressively trained chimp is only performing individual tricks, devoid of any social or ecological import.[4]

The remainder of *Ant* explores this process of myth-making and suggests some reasons for the precise images and values that have been attached to ants at various times and in various places. The rest of this chapter, however, is devoted to a summary of the contemporary scientific understanding of ants: the stories that are told by myrmecologists today.[5]

The animal kingdom is divided into successively smaller categories, which as they decrease in size reflect a greater degree of similarity and presumed evolutionary connection between their members. Phyla are the largest groups, which are then successively divided into classes, orders, families, genera, and finally into species. Insects are one class of the phylum Arthropoda. (Non-insectan arthropods include crustaceans and spiders.) The class Insecta is made up of various orders, including Coleoptera (beetles) and Lepidoptera (butterflies and moths). The order Hymenoptera contains ants, as well as their evolutionary cousins, the bees and wasps. Termites, although often referred to as 'white ants' have long been assigned to a different order, the Isoptera, which they share with their less loveable relations, cockroaches. Within the order Hymenoptera, one family – Formicidae – contains all the true ants. Ants are easy to recognize compared with many other insects. All are the same basic shape and have a characteristic kink in their ever-busy antennae. The Formicidae are split down into around three hundred genera, some of which have informal descriptive names such as sugar ants, bulldog ants or meat ants. Individual species vary in size between 0.7 millimetres and 3 centimetres in length.

At the time of writing, the latest count of ant species was 11,006. Although this represents a tiny proportion of known

Frontal view of worker ant (*Paratrechina* sp.) showing the antennal kink characteristic of all modern ants.

insect species (about 750,000, of which most are beetles), the combined weight of all living ants has been estimated to constitute half the mass of all extant insects. This figure, out of all proportion to the number of insect species, shows the success of ants in exploiting a variety of habitats around the world: just about everywhere apart from the polar regions.

Virtually all of the ants one sees are infertile female workers, engaged in functions such as foraging, nest maintenance or defence, and tending the young. Inside the nest there are also sexual forms, both male and female. At some point, these ants will fly up into the air and mate; these are the swarms of winged ants that are commonly seen in late summer. Most will be eaten by birds, and the males have no function at all in the colony beyond this brief task of fertilization. A few fecundated females, however, return to earth to found a new colony. Each will shed

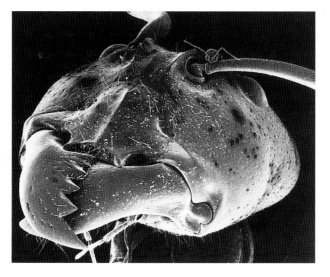

An entire colony of *Brachymyrmex* (top right, behind antenna) would fit into the head of the large Bornean carpenter ant filling most of this scanning electron micrograph.

Dramatic size differences between ants can also be observed in real life. Here, in Auguste Forel's *The Social World of the Ants Compared with That of Man* (1928), seemingly unmatched species are locked in battle.

An alate (winged) queen sets off to found her colony, accompanied by tiny workers from the nest where she was born clinging to her legs.

her wings, digest the muscles that powered her short flight, and lay her first batch of eggs. She may have to leave the young from time to time in order to search for food; if need be, she may even consume some of the eggs or larvae in order to sustain herself. The larvae pupate, and emerge in the adult form. Once raised, this first generation of workers can take over the care of subsequent broods, leaving the queen to the business of egg-laying for the remainder of her life.

As the nest matures, the number of workers increases, their labour becomes divided and the nest grows still more. When it has grown to a sufficient size, the queen will produce sexual forms ready for the next mating season. Since fertilization, she has been storing sperm and releasing them one or several at a time with each egg produced. Now, she releases some unfertilized eggs, which will become the males. Sexual females are produced, like their infertile sisters, from fertilized eggs. They are turned into a sexual form simply by being fed a different diet. In almost all species, the colony will last as long as the queen is alive, generally between five and twenty years. When the queen dies, the colony gradually declines until the last worker dies out.

There are many variations on this basic life cycle. Some nests are founded by multiple queens, of which all but one may later be eliminated; some gradually branch out with new queens and workers to form satellite branches of the larger 'supercolony'. Other nests may adopt supernumerary queens. Queens of some species take workers with them when they found a new nest; this process is known as swarming. In other species the queen is altogether incapable of raising that critical first brood by herself. In this case, she may invade another nest on a temporary or permanent basis, using its workers to raise her young alongside, or instead of, their own.

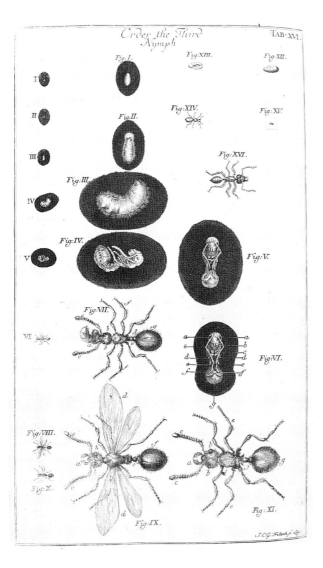

A very early depiction of the ant's life-cycle in John Swammerdam's *The Book of Nature, or, The History of Insects* (1758).

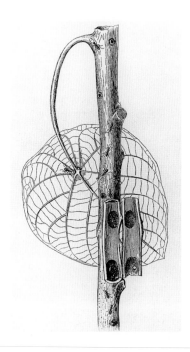

Ants' nests are found in all kinds of places including inside plants, such as this *Endospermum formicarum* inhabited by a colony of *Camponotus quadriceps* in an illustration of 1910.

Army ants, found in the tropics, have no physical base to their colony at all. They simply hang in a cluster overnight, forming a bivouac around their queen. When it is time to hunt, the whole colony goes on the march, swarming across the ground and eating anything in its path, until night falls once again. These ants, from several widely separated genera, are, however, in the minority. Most species have a fixed base, a nest around which their existence revolves. At its centre there is generally an enclosed dwelling constructed by the ants, the place to which all the ants return at night and at the heart of which the queen shelters, producing young. Just outside the nest, there is often an area known as the midden, which is the refuse heap of the colony. Extending all around this area is the territory of the nest.

Ants often live in symbiosis with the plants they inhabit, offering them protection in return for shelter. Here a Papua New Guinean epiphyte is inhabited by *Iridomyrmex* ants, in an illustration of 1910.

The nest contains a number of different castes and ants in various stages of maturity. The workers perform a wide variety of tasks. The nurses tend the eggs, larvae and pupae. Many researchers have noted how they carry them off in times of threat, or move them from one part of the nest to another over the course of the day, in order to maintain them at the correct temperature as the nest warms and then cools with the passage of the sun. They lick the young constantly, coating them with

Ant hill belonging to wood ants. During the day, workers are busy maintaining the hill.

antiseptic chemicals that inhibit the growth of bacteria within the nest.

Meanwhile, maintenance workers gather up pieces of dirt and use them to mend or build the nest. Patrollers inspect the nest and its surroundings, checking the ants they encounter to see if they are foreigners. It seems that they also pick out places to forage, and the routes to get there. Foragers, as their name implies, go out searching for food, or are recruited to exploit the food sources located by their nest-mates. They tend to follow trails made by their predecessors between the nest and food sources. Food is shared rapidly by the whole nest by mutual regurgitation, known as trophallaxis. Midden workers tend the refuse heap outside the nest, and may move it from place to place. Soldiers protect the nest and may also engage in aggressive behaviour, whether against other colonies of the same or different species or against other insects altogether.

Keeping control of the colony's territory is essential, as it yields the food necessary to maintain the population. As the colony grows, so it must extend its foraging territory. When the

Ants can squirt formic acid to ward off threats, giving them their characteristic odour when disturbed. From Auguste Forel's *Social World of the Ants Compared with That of Man* (1928).

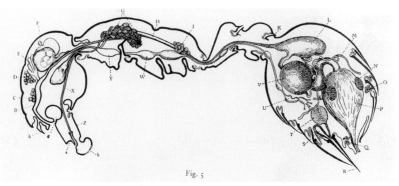

Fig. 5

Trophallaxis is facilitated by a crop or 'social stomach' (L) from which ants can regurgitate food. From Auguste Forel, *Social World of the Ants Compared with That of Man* (1928).

territories of adjacent colonies meet, battle occurs. The colony's soldiers fight by stinging or spraying one another with poison, as well as by wrestling and chopping with their mandibles. A frequent choice of poison spray is formic acid, which lends many species' nests their distinctive scent when disturbed. This odour, reminiscent of urine, gives ants their Middle English name: pismire. Ants often enter into conflict with other insects as well, especially termites. Some species will even raid another ants' nest, stealing its young for food. An evolutionary arms race keeps the ecological balance between competing species; when ants are introduced into a new location they can wipe out native species unused to the battle tactics of the newcomers.

According to some researchers, the nest itself may be regarded as going through a process of maturation, as evidenced in its collective behaviour. Following a 'timid' period after establishment, it may go through an aggressive phase, seeking out conflict with its neighbours, probably in an effort to expand. More mature colonies coexist more peacefully with nearby nests, keeping to their own foraging paths and avoiding confrontation.

Certain species of ant go beyond direct conflict for food; they raid other nests for ants to act as their slaves (a phenomenon

referred to by contemporary myrmecologists as dulosis). Many steal pupae rather than adults; pupae can be imbued with their masters' nest odour and when they emerge they behave exactly as though they were working for their own species. Some slave-making ants depend utterly on their imported aliens, even to the extent of having no worker castes of their own and being unable to feed themselves. One of the most common slave relationships, between a species of red ant, *Polyergus rufescens*, and its black victims, *Formica fusca*, inspired many nineteenth century writers to speak unselfconsciously of 'Negro ants'. Others, finding the thought of slavery in the animal world abominable, have insisted that the aliens are not 'slaves' but 'auxiliaries', as Pierre Huber did as early as 1810. Abraham Lincoln took the opposite tack, suggesting that humans should rise above ant

In a phenomenon known as social parasitism, a single queen can intrude into a colony of another species, kill the host queen, and then use the host workers to rear her own brood. Here two species of the genus *Lasius* are involved.

morality (albeit attributing something like that primitive Mac brainpower to black slaves):

> The ant, who has toiled and dragged a crumb to his nest, will furiously defend the fruit of his labor, against whatever robber assails him. So plain, that the most dumb and stupid slave that ever toiled for a master, does constantly know that he is wronged.[6]

Other ants have modes of sustenance more acceptable to human reporters. Harvesting ants, which probably inspired Solomon to recommend that the sluggard should 'go to the ant . . . consider her ways and be wise', collect up seeds from their arid environments and store them in the nest. Many researchers have observed that they actually chew off the radicle, the germinating part of the seed, to prevent its growth within the nest. If the seeds become damp, they are moved to the outside of the nest in order to dry. When needed, the seeds are chewed and moistened until they can be used for food.

Another famous ant lifestyle is based upon aphids and other, similar, small bugs (Homoptera). Aphids are able to suck juice out of plants using their sharp mouth parts. The ants, in turn, stroke the bugs with their antennae, an act of solicitation which induces them to secrete a droplet of 'honeydew' for the ant. The precise manner of this exchange causes some disquiet to Woody Allen, as Z in the film *AntZ*. When asked 'Don't you want your aphid beer?' he protests 'Call me crazy but I have a thing about drinking from the anus of another creature.' More decorously, Victorian writers were fond of comparing ants' aphids to cows, kept for their milk. However described, this relationship is just one example of the many symbiotic relationships in which ant species engage, both with other

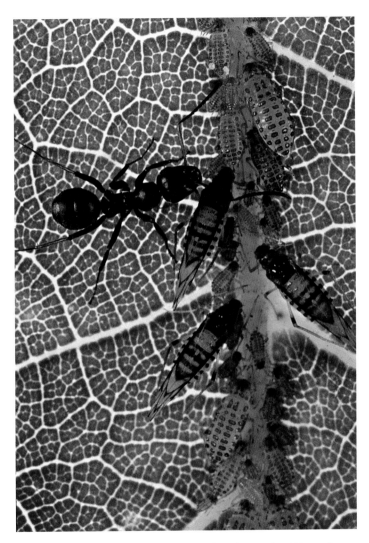

Ant milking aphids on the leaf of a walnut tree. She induces each aphid to emit a droplet of honeydew by stroking it with her antennae.

insects and with plants. In this particular case, the aphids enjoy the protection from predators afforded by the ants; some ants even go so far as to enclose them safely in their own nests.

Honey ants store food in their own relatives' bodies. These desert-dwelling species feed up selected workers during times of plenty, until their bodies are distended balloons of sugary liquid. These workers then hang from the roof of the nest until, in time of dearth, the contents of their crops are required by the colony and they feed the others by trophallaxis. Sometimes the strategy does not work, for Australian Aboriginals are skilled at finding and digging them up; the ants are considered a sweet delicacy.

Leafcutter ants cultivate a fungus, which they use for food. As their name suggests, they gather fragments of foliage (so successfully that they are an agricultural pest in their home, the American tropics), and transport them back to the nest. Here the leaves are impregnated with a fungus, which is left to grow until ready for consumption. Comparisons with human farming have come easily to observers of this phenomenon.

From slave-makers to gardeners, ants each have 20 to 40 different acts in their repertoire of behaviour, depending on the species. According to some, the exact repertoire is tightly linked to the caste of the ant concerned. Others see a greater degree of behavioural flexibility in each individual, allowing her the ability to exercise a greater proportion of the total acts exhibited by the population as a whole.

Coordinating the functions of the nest members – of which there can be two million or more – requires a reliable system of communication. To find and retrieve food with maximum efficiency, foragers need to be able to recruit their fellow workers to good sources. They must be able to recognize their own nest mates and distinguish them from potentially hostile foreigners.

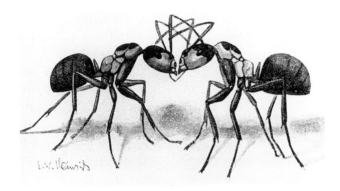

Antennal communication, using the sense of touch and especially that of smell, is crucial to ants' organized behaviour. From Forel's *Social World of the Ants* (1928).

If enemies are detected they need to be able to signal their presence to their own kind, recruiting some to the battle and others to the task of saving eggs, larvae and pupae. All these tasks and more are completed in the main through chemical communication – pheromones. Ants produce ten or twenty different chemicals to signal specific requests and warnings, passing them through physical contact or leaving them behind as chemical trails. Apparently complex tasks can be carried out through a simple reinforcement system. Weaver ants, for example, join together to bend two leaves together and glue them in place. The 'decision' to pick a particular leaf for this team effort is set in motion by a single worker; if she succeeds in bending a leaf slightly, she releases a 'success' pheromone, which recruits another to the task. If she too finds the leaf bendable, she will reinforce the signal with her own, and so on in a positive feedback loop. In a like manner, ants will gradually carve out an optimal homeward route from a good food source. Pheromones also exercise more long-term control: those secreted by the queen prevent the sexual maturation of the workers, while those produced by soldiers limit the numbers of their caste to a level suitable for the colony as a whole. Hölldobler and Wilson

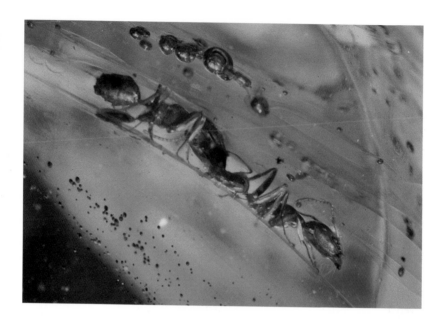

Ants of the Lower Miocene in Dominican amber (about 20 million years old). One is holding the other's abdomen with its jaws.

summarize colony communication thus: 'Ants, like humans, to put it in a nutshell, succeed because they talk so well.'[7]

Ants preserved in amber show, rather beautifully, that they have been abundant in Northern Europe in something very like their modern form for 25 to 40 million years. It has puzzled many, including Darwin, how ants have reached this modern form, with its highly developed form of social life. Until the 1930s myrmecologists got their best answers by looking at living wasps. There are no ants that live independently, but there are some species of wasp that do.

Different solitary wasp species raise their offspring in different ways. Some leave food with their eggs, ready for the larvae when they hatch. Others continue to bring food after they have hatched. Still other species bring their progeny live, paralyzed prey, or prey that has been softened and made more edible in pellet form. Early twentieth-century researchers saw these as steps towards a social interaction between the generations.[8] Moreover, they posited that in order to make best use of available food resources, back in time the female had facultatively switched from one of these behaviours to another. These acquired behaviours, they concluded, subsequently and gradually became fixed forms of life for future generations, culminating in the mother's dependence on a trans-generational worker caste (i.e. her daughters) to maintain reproductive success. This, entomologists concluded, was how primitive, solitary wasp-ants had gradually acquired a socialized form of life, and hence evolved into modern ants.

Ants still found in Australia provide a tantalizing glimpse of primitive sociality, just as its marsupials seem to illustrate a very undeveloped form of mammalian anatomy. These ants maintain rather small colonies, and their workers are not

Three species of extant primitive ant. The one on the left is from Madagascar, the others from Australia. Note their unusual anatomical forms. From Forel's *Social World of the Ants*.

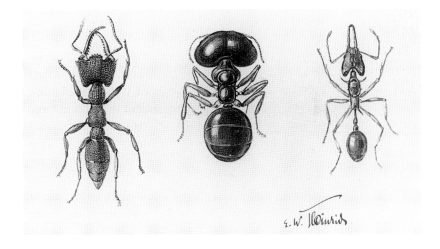

ε. W. Heinrich

25

divided into specialized castes for care of the young, fighting, foraging and so on. Nor do they seem to communicate much amongst themselves, but forage for food individually, like solitary wasps.

Meanwhile, the 'waisted' appearance of modern wasps and ants, along with other anatomical similarities, also suggest a close evolutionary relationship between the two families. From this and other morphological information, entomologists predicted the physical characteristics that they expected to find in the earliest ants, during the transitional period from solitary insects into their social form. In 1966, while searching on their local beach, a retired couple from New Jersey found the oldest amber-preserved specimens yet. Fulfilling myrmecologists' expectations, the new fossils shared some key characteristics with modern ants, and some with wasps. They therefore placed them in a new genus: *Sphecomyrma*, meaning 'wasp ant'. For entomologists, it was as exciting as the discovery of the missing link between primates and human beings. They speculated that *Sphecomyrma* lived much like the Australian primitives. Inside the amber they had caught a glimpse of the birth of society, 100 to 120 million years ago.

These facts, then, represent the current scientific consensus about ants. But they may also be seen as myths, just like Plato's and Pliny's. I do not mean to suggest that one should consider them fiction. There is, however, no single correct way of studying ants; like everything else in our universe, they can be described on multiple levels. At various times, investigators have chosen different aspects of ant life to study, including anatomy, classification, evolution, physiology, psychological attributes and social behaviour. These choices, neither right nor wrong in themselves, have simply reflected the preoccupations

of the observers at the time they were made: collecting, dissecting, telling origin stories, knowing the human mind, understanding crowd behaviour.

More than this, the language and models we use to try and capture and explain any natural phenomenon are drawn from our culture ('queens', 'sisters'), and reflect something about our own perspectives at the same time as they describe the outside world. As this chapter began by remarking, even modern, 'factual' myrmecologists are drawn to mythic language in describing their findings. Rather than seeing all this as a limitation on scientific objectivity, *Ant* suggests that by understanding the cultural contingencies of science, we gain a much richer and fuller picture of it. In the following chapter, a little digging beneath the surface reveals some possible reasons why myrmecologists consistently describe the tiny in such magnified terms.

One way to study ants: observation of their behaviour in nature.

Another way to study ants: scanning electron microscopy (SEM) of their physiology.

2 Ants as Minions

Looking down on the tiny world of the ants, humans have long been tempted to imagine that the colonies they see are kingdoms at their own disposal. The Ancient Greeks' mythical loyal soldiers, the Myrmidons, share the root of their name with ants – the same base from which we get several English ant-related words such as myrmecology or the genus *Myrmecia*. Ants march together with such astonishing organization and indefatigable persistence that the Ancient Greeks saw in them the qualities of the most desirable or dreaded troops, depending on whose side they were fighting.

A veteran of the Spanish-American and American Civil Wars, Henry McCook, was also fascinated by ants. McCook had raised a division of volunteers in Illinois, acting as their captain and their chaplain. But for him, ants were the ideal army. He described how ants would be the perfect minions to command:

> . . . our mountain mound-builder . . . [ants] remind us of the militia organization of our earlier frontier States – Ohio, for example, which made every adult male, not disqualified by age or otherwise, subject to military duty. Indeed, such is, in theory, the relation of all citizens of the American republic to the general government. Among our ants that duty is never dodged. There are

Marching Through Georgia

'Marching Through Georgia' (1957) portrays ants as an invading Union army of the American Civil War.

no desertions. Lazy, cowardly and skulking ants one does not see. With heartiest good-will the call to service is met . . .[1]

There exists a variety of ways in which humans indulge their dream of the formic army. Some, like McCook, enjoy the opportunity to experience a comparative sense of grandeur over their tiny subjects. There is also a sense in which ants exemplify the massed power of the individually insignificant, providing a comforting alternate reality for the downtrodden. Others take consolation from the thought of empathetically entering the little world of the individual ant, who, even on her own, functions as the archetypal fairy-tale victor over apparently superior forces. What these visions share – from entomologists' reminiscences, to children's fiction, to ancient myth – is a fantasy about ants based on power.

ARMIES OF THE INSIGNIFICANT

Few people get to command armies, but everyone can dream of being on the right end of the order-giving process. Hence the pleasure of an army of toy soldiers, a battalion of model Myrmidons in the original Greek sense. The fantasy of a king-dom of ants under one's rule amounts to much the same thing. The fantasist becomes, comparatively, a giant in his own world; a hectored child in the house can enter the garden and find there a realm in which he is gigantically, incontestably godlike.

Auguste Forel was such a child; he was born in 1848 in the Swiss countryside near Lausanne to a well-connected and wealthy family. Eventually Auguste was to become an influen-tial psychiatrist and an internationally recognized expert upon ants. As a child, however, he was timid and sickly, lonely and miserable. He detested his mother's over-protective, neurotic Calvinist company. 'Apart from visits to my grandparents', he wrote in later life, 'I was cut off from all human intercourse. My mother would not even let me go into the garden alone.' He found his escape among the ants, whose social life began to fascinate him from the age of six. He watched colonies of three different species around the house, feeding them 'lovingly . . .

with bread, sugar and so forth'.[2] It would be no exaggeration to say that the little Auguste loved his ants. He was moved to despair when his favourite nest was raided by an army of red ants, and angrily poured boiling water over the invaders, but to no avail. A little later, having been taught some of the classics, he began writing a Homeric epic, 'Wars of the Ants', a '*Fourmiad*' in which the ant-hill building *Formica pratensis*, the meadow ant, played the part of the Greeks, while the blood-red robber ants, *Formica sanguinea*, were the deceitful Trojans. Forel's notebooks, which he kept from an early age, are full of sketches, notes and coded script, all of which show how intently he absorbed himself into the tiny realm of the ants as an escape from his mother and the 'continual surfeit of the Bible and religious doctrine'.[3] He had found in the ants' kingdom a miniature *topos*, which though part of the larger world seemed to him to be independent of it. It was autonomous and utopian, and crowned him as its sovereign.

Forel was by no means unique in his formic consolation. As

a child in the 1930s, E. O. Wilson was shuffled from place to place by his separated parents. This nomadic existence made him, like Forel, lonely and socially anxious. Now the world's best-known myrmecologist, he suggests that 'loneliness in a beautiful environment might be a good if risky way to create a . . . field biologist'. [4] This was certainly true for him: instead of making human friends, he too found comradeship amongst the mythic armies of the minuscule. 'I rescued bits of Spanish moss . . . They were my friends . . . I kept harvester ants in a jar of sand under my bed . . . I discovered fairy tales. . .'.[5]

The 1960s Spanish children's book *Ladis and the Ant* might almost be a fictionalized account of Forel's or Wilson's childhood, featuring as it does a colony of ants acting as saviour of its unhappy protagonist. An eight-year-old boy, Ladis, is sent away to the countryside for the summer on account of his poor health. He takes with him his timidity and sense of inferiority; like Solomon's ants he is described in the very first paragraph as 'not strong'. It is only when Ladis is magically reduced to the size of an ant by a friendly queen, and becomes familiar with the interior of the ants' nest, that he learns to be at ease and starts getting better. The ant carries him like an obedient horse and anxiously tells Ladis 'You might suddenly take it into your head to make yourself grow inside the anthill, and destroy us all.' Ladis learns to wrestle with the ants, discovering that he can defeat them if he grabs their antennae. Ladis' new-found sense of power and confidence lasts even when he is back among humans: 'how lucky he was to be able to do just what he liked, whenever he liked'. The memory of his personal army sustains him.[6]

Thus the massed power of individually insignificant ants is a source of hope to the impotent. Moreover, this vision of ants is shared by a variety of cultures. In Vietnam there is a saying, 'con

Another boy who found courage through commanding an army of ants: Ladis. An illustration from José Maria Sanchez-Silva, *Ladis and the Ant* (1968).

kien cong con vua'; by sticking together the tiny ants can carry the elephant. The writer Le Ly Hayslip has described how this saying took on additional significance during the Vietnam War: 'The American elephant could rage and stomp the Vietnamese anthill, but time and weight of numbers guaranteed that it would eventually be the *ants*, not the elephant, who danced on the bones of the victims.'[7] Vietnamese literature from the war compared Vietnamese teamwork with communal insect labour, while the US military were likened to mere swarms of insects without virtues: flies and locusts. It is therefore no surprise that although the Vietnamese have oxen, their cliché asserts that someone is 'kien cang' – strong as an ant.

TOYING WITH SCALE

When people brought mathematics to bear upon the fantasy of formic minions, they concluded that having an army of ants would be even better than an army of miniature humans (or, conversely, that an army of giant ants would win over humans). Henry McCook's calculations made ants seem even more attractive as agents under his control. He wondered how ants' nests compared with the Ancient Egyptians' greatest achievements, the pyramids, and calculated how the volume of each edifice (ant mound and pyramid) related to the bodily size of its builders. 'Man's bulk to his building is as 1 to 12½ millions', he concluded; 'the ant's bulk to her building is as 1 to 5800 millions. A simple calculation will show how greatly this exhibits the comparative superiority of the insect.'[8]

On reading McCook, the Belgian playwright and author Maurice Maeterlinck commented that compared to anthills, London and New York would be 'no more than villages'. He went on to describe the most common assessment of ant-human scale: 'When we see ants . . . carrying . . . with the greatest ease, with the tips of their mandibles . . . pine needles or fragments of wood which to us would represent beams or posts which two or three men could barely handle, we believe them to be endowed with a muscular force . . . eight or ten times as great as our own.'[9] Truly, it would be wonderful to have such soldiers under one's command.

The little Auguste Forel, while dreaming of ants, toyed with scale in order to triumph, mentally, over his enemies. He used to imagine that he had a magic balloon that could alter the scale of things around him, putting his own personal tyrants in their place.

> If [I] put one of my pet ants into the balloon, allowed the latter to expand, and then opened it, the ant was magnified in proportion, and had now become a giant creature, able to tear things to pieces and swallow them. If, on the other hand, a nasty little boy, or one of my enemies, was placed in the balloon, he was diminished accordingly. So everything happened as I wished.[10]

Such calculations reveal another important facet of ant representation. Leaving aside the massed aspect of ant allies, there is comfort to be found in their scale alone. The myths of many cultures relate victory for the poor man over the prince, the boy over the man, the David over the Goliath. Ants perfectly fulfil this role in art and literature, signifying the success, against the odds, of the 'little guy'. The Indonesian version of the game 'scissors, paper, stone' illustrates the point well. In Indonesia, the three categories are ant, human and elephant. Though the human can trample the ant, and the elephant squash the human, ant triumphs over elephant since, in this game, the elephant cannot stand the ticklish sensation of having it inside its ear. In this mould also comes Frank Sinatra's ant with his [sic] 'high hopes' about moving the rubber tree plant; within this tradition the very unlikeliness of the feat justifies his optimism. By a curious coincidence, when George Bush Jr named North Korea as part of the post-9/11 'axis of evil', the North Koreans reached for a similar formic metaphor to describe their heroic conflict with the Americans. Amongst other animal comparisons, they likened their efforts to those of 'an ant trying to topple an oak tree'. The us newspaper reporting this explained to its readers 'ordinary North Koreans are so isolated from the outside world that they don't realize how unrealistic these analogies are'.[11]

William Blake describes a scaled-down empathy with the insignificant in 'A Dream' from *Songs of Innocence*. In it, the poet prophetically dreams that a lost ant is guided home to her family by a glow-worm. The structure of the poem suggests that his strong sense of identification with the ant is divinely inspired, for it begins with angels round the poet's bed weaving the dream for him, implying that they too offer a lamp for his path and safe shepherding homeward. Blake's well-known antipathy for the values of the enlightenment also found support in the insect world, whose miniature qualities put the new philosophy in its place: 'The emmet's inch and eagle's mile/Make lame Philosophy to smile.'

Blake's most famous meditation on scale hints at an explanation for the comfort so often found in the realm of the tiny. In 'Auguries of Innocence' he writes of the way in which a contemplation of the miniature can bring about a sense of containing the complexities of the world in safety and peace:

To see a World in a Grain of Sand
And Heaven in a Wild Flower,
Hold Infinity in the palm of your hand
And Eternity in an hour.

This, suggests poet and critic Susan Stewart, is the essence of our fascination with the tiny.[12] She claims, persuasively, that miniaturized commodities represent human attempts to bring the world under their own control. By creating tiny versions of reality, we contain it safely within ourselves; we personalize the wider world, interiorize it. Indeed, artificial ants' nests –

An early 19th-century bell-style artificial ants' nest, suitable for wood ants.

M. HUBER'S FORMICARY FOR WOOD-ANTS.

An early 19th-
century cabinet-
style artificial ants'
nest, suitable for
mason ants.

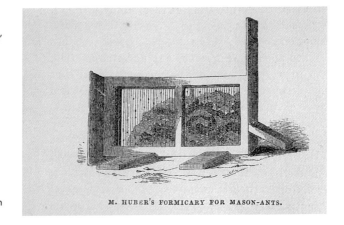

M. HUBER'S FORMICARY FOR MASON-ANTS.

Ant Farms® toys
such as this one
remain popular
among children in
the USA.

popular since the nineteenth century – are a living version of the dolls' houses that Stewart uses to exemplify her theory.

Forel and Wilson's childhood experiences are in line with a tradition identified by Stewart, the heyday of which was in nineteenth-century books and art. In these texts and pictures, images of nature blend with fairy tales, and a playful attitude towards scale is used to explore the world, and finally to reassure the reader about their place within it. Lewis Carroll's Alice is the most famous example, famously encountering a giant caterpillar on her size-changing travels. Other writers concentrated wholly on insects. One beautiful example of this genre is *The Population of an Old Pear-Tree*, published in English in 1870.

The book opens with the author in 'blue spirits'; he goes out into the fields to escape the oppression of his everyday life, and soon falls asleep. He is woken by the sound of angry voices, complaining that his feet have crushed many of their number – and all at once, his senses become 'marvellously acute'. He is able to see insects face to face, the same size as himself. The narrator's first sight is a terrifying one: he looks up to see a giant, ravenous spider descending towards him. He is saved by a fly, who becomes entrapped in the spider's web and distracts her attention. Unable to escape, the fly becomes the spider's hapless victim, but not before a 'loathsome little parasite' has managed to detach itself from the fly's back and make good its retreat.

The engravings, depicting this event and the narrator's subsequent encounters with insects, are fascinating in the way they oscillate between same-size and real-life perspectives. The first three lead the reader through from an ordinary perspective and into the world where the spider is a frightening giant. But this perspective is not retained for the rest of the book. In some, the narrator is the same size as the insects; in others, he is clearly bigger. In the same way, he switches between two kinds of self-

Shrinking to the size of an ant, the reader of E. van Bruyssel's *The Population of an Old Pear Tree* (1870) from which this illustration comes is temporarily terrorized by a spider.

Other sights in the insect realm, however, charm the miniaturized reader.

perception in relation to the insects. The incident with the spider, the fly and the parasite humbles yet comforts the writer; he murmurs to himself 'This lowest parasite, fallen from a fly's wing, perhaps had his own vermin preying on himself. In space there is star beyond star; on earth, one atom is lost in another atom.' His moment of epiphany goes on 'I stopped, confounded by this overwhelming thought; here began my initiation. The character of the meadow had changed, and I henceforward called it my book of devotion.'[13] Yet holding in memory the

A vision of ants as soldiers reminds the reader of the potential power that comes by massing the tiny.

A recapitulation
of comparative
scale reasserts
the superiority
of the reader.

larger scale from which he came, the narrator can also entertain
the notion of being ruler of the insect minions:

> Divided, they fall a prey to the strong; yet, united, their
> power is invincible. Hercules, the conqueror of the
> Erymanthian boar, would have been put to flight by a
> legion of ants.[14]

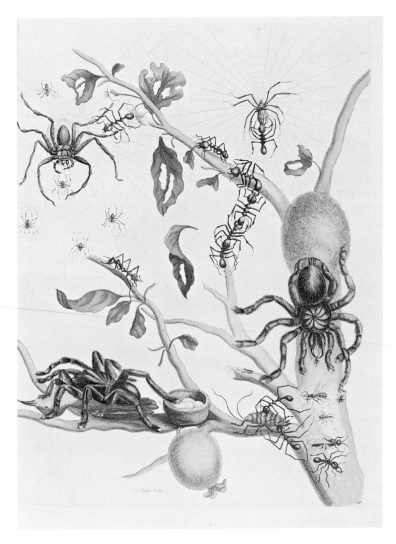

Spiders and ants in a hand-coloured engraving from Maria Sibylla Merian's *Dissertation sur . . . des insectes de Surinam* (The Hague, 1726).

Being able to enter the two perspectives at will allows the narrative to switch between a safe enclosure within and superiority over the miniature realm: the twin poles of the miniaturization game.

The film *Microcosmos* (1996), which photographs insects close up and in intense colour – like Maria Sibylla Merian's jewel-like insect engravings of the early eighteenth century – is a piece of representation that toys with the viewer's sense of scale. In this world of the miniature, time seems to last longer than the one hour of film; one is drawn right into the experiential realm of insects, while maintaining a sense of astonishment at their close up appearance. One constantly shifts between the world of the human and the insect; each transition brings with it either a sense of wonder or a sensation of grandeur.

CREATION MYTHS AND OTHER ANCIENT ANT LORE

Like dreams of commanding an ant army, creation myths involving ants play with concepts about power. They weigh up the relative positions of humans, the gods, and the rest of nature. For William Petty in the seventeenth century, creation showed that 'there are beings within . . . the orb of the fixed Starrs . . . which do [more] incomparably excell man in the sense of dignity and infirmity than man doth excell the vilest insect'.[15] But not all cultures share his sense of divinely imposed humility through contemplation of the insect realm. Many use such myths to reinforce the opposite attitude: the fantasy of omnipotence.

In the latter vein, Ovid describes the creation of the original Myrmidons. Juno in her jealousy had sent a plague that wiped out every animal and then every human on the island of Aegina. Only the king, Aeacus, remained. He pleaded with Zeus to restore his people, and, as he reported to his friend Cephalus, was answered in an unexpected way:

> By chance there grew by the place where I stood an oak with wide-spreading branches, sacred to Jupiter. I observed a troop of ants busy with their labour, carrying minute grains in their mouths, and following one another in a line up the trunk of the tree. Observing their numbers with admiration, I said, 'Give me, O father, citizens as numerous as these and replenish my empty city.' . . . Night came on and took possession of my frame . . . The tree stood before me in my dreams, with its numerous branches all covered with living, moving creatures. It seemed to shake its limbs and throw down over the ground a multitude of those industriousness grain-gathering animals, which appeared to gain in size, and grow larger and larger, and by and by to stand erect, lay aside their superfluous legs and their black colour, and finally to assume the human form. Then I awoke . . . I saw a multitude of men such as I had seen in my dream, and

Aeacus watches his army of Myrmidons metamorphose from ants to humans in a drawing by Stanley William Hayter (1942).

46

they were passing in procession in the same manner. While I gazed with wonder and delight they approached, and kneeling hailed me as their king.[16]

Aeacus named his new subjects Myrmidons from the word 'ant' (*myrmex*). They turned out to be fiercely and doggedly loyal, not only to Aeacus but also to his exiled son Peleus, and Peleus' son Achilles. In Troy, where the Myrmidons fought for Achilles, they regained some of the ant-like characteristics lost in their initial transformation. They fought wearing black armour, and carried black shields, moving as one mass just like soldier ants:

> . . . the ranks dressed closer when they heard their prince. Their helmets and their bossed shields were as tightly packed as the blocks of stone that a mason fits together . . . They stood so close together, shield to shield, helmet to helmet, man to man, that when they moved their heads the glittering peaks of their plumed helmets met.[17]

Interestingly, Homer compares the Myrmidons' bloodthirsty demeanour in battle to that of the ants' cousins, the wasps:

> Picture a horde of wasps pouring out from the side of a road . . . a public menace. No sooner does a traveller come by and unwittingly disturb them than they are up in arms and one and all fly out to fight for their little ones. That was the spirit in which the Myrmidons poured out from behind the ships, with an indescribable din . . . They fell on the Trojans in a body . . .[18]

Aeacus' Myrmidons were the perfect personal army, specially created, under complete control and totally loyal to their master.

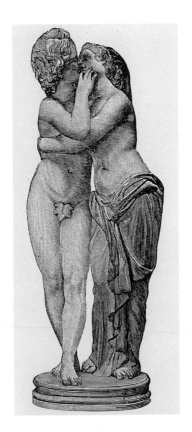

This kiss between Cupid and Psyche provoked punishment by Venus; though the ants tried to help Psyche they did so in vain.

Another Greek myth exploring this fantasy is the story of Cupid and Psyche. Psyche was being punished by Venus, who decreed that she could only regain her husband Cupid if she performed a trial of industry and diligence. Psyche was led to a storehouse containing a vast heap of mixed grains, and ordered to sort them into separate heaps by evening. She sat in silent consternation, but all was not lost:

This 1800 engraving accompanied a re-telling of Aesop's 'The Dove and the Ant'. 'The most important actions are often performed by the most unlikely instruments', counselled the author.

While she sat despairing, Cupid stirred up a little ant, a native of the fields, to take compassion on her. The leader of the anthill, followed by whole hosts of his six-legged subjects, approached the heap, and with the utmost diligence taking grain by grain, they separated the pile, sorting each kind to its parcel; and when it was all done, they vanished out of sight in a moment.[19]

Aesop's fable about the ant and the dove also explores the fantasy of employing these miniaturized powers of the world as one's personal army.[20] In this story, a thirsty ant is swept away by a rivulet of water, but is saved by a dove who breaks off a twig and throws it for the ant to climb onto. Later on, the ant sees a bird-catcher preparing to trap the dove. It stings the hunter's foot; he drops his limed twigs and scares off the dove. The miniaturization and hence personalization of nature's powers is a potent way to construct the traditional and ubiquitous tale about the triumph of the underdog.

A traditional story from Southern China inverts the key elements in these Greek myths. Rather than having the gods provide ants to serve and save the story's protagonist, this Chinese tale has fate provide freakish salvation for the main character, who subsequently turns into a host of ants. The story concerns a man with a nagging wife. In order to persuade his wife that he can provide for the family, he claims that he has a supernatural sense of smell. The emperor soon hears of his supposed powers, and invites him to demonstrate them in finding his missing jade seal. Trapped, and expected to perform a feat of which he knows he is incapable, the man mutters a phrase of despair. By a remarkable coincidence, this sounds like the name of two guilty courtiers, who immediately confess to him the location of the stolen seal. Next, the empress asks him to divine by smell what she has hidden in a cloth bag. Again, the man despairs; the exits are guarded and he knows he has no hope of guessing. This time he cries out regarding his own predicament 'Alas, the bagged cat dies!' only to find himself cheered, for the empress has indeed hidden a kitten in the bag (which has unfortunately died during the course of the trial). All the courtiers declare that the man must be a god, so they take hold of him and toss him high into the heavens. They throw him so high that when he falls back down he is dashed into dust, and each piece of dust turns into an ant. This, the story concludes, is why ants can sniff out food however carefully it is hidden. [21]

SUBVERSIVE ANTS?

Aesop is well known for having written a fable showing the prudence of the ant. But other of his tales give a different slant on the Ancient Greek perspective on ants, hinting at a possible connection with Aeacus' or Psyche's fantasy of commanding a Myrmidon army. One such is very brief:

A man who saw a ship sink with all hands protested against the injustice of the gods: because there was one impious person on board, he said, they had destroyed the innocent as well. As he spoke he was bitten by one of a swarm of ants which had attacked him; and, though only one had attacked him, he trampled on them all. At this Hermes smote him with his staff, saying: 'Will you not allow the gods to judge men as you judge ants?'[22]

This tale might hastily be interpreted along the same lines as Petty's dictum: don't consider yourself mighty on earth, because you look just as insignificant to the gods as insects appear to you. But Aesop – or the original author – was not a Protestant moralist, and the character of Hermes in other fables by him casts doubt on the nature of his justice.

The story would feel very different if it were Zeus who was doing the judging. Through the moral implausibility of his judgement, Hermes may in fact implicitly commend the man for his opportunistic exercise of power. This does seem to be the tone in which Aesop describes the ant in his 'just so' story about its creation: originally the ant was a farmer who went around stealing his neighbours' produce.[23] Zeus transformed him into the first ant – and in this form 'he' has continued to behave the same way to this very day.

Another of Hermes' exploits suggests a subversive-miniature interpretation of the created order. When Zeus had finished creating humans, he gave Hermes the task of giving them their intelligence. Hermes used just one vessel to measure out the

Honey ant chocolates, using two different species: *Melophorus bagoti* and *Camponotus* sp.

Aboriginal family in Australia digging for honey ants.

same amount for everyone: it filled the small men perfectly, but big men were half empty, and so turned out stupid.[24] The small are again exalted and identified with the reader, while the large are ridiculed, just as Stewart suggests.

Honey ants (see Chapter 1) seem like very literal human servants from the insect world, but like some of Aesop's ants, they may in fact be more subversive. Hanging in their underground nests, these ants provide tasty morsels for humans who have the skill to find them buried amid the dusty landscape – no easy task for the uninitiated. Honey ants are a popular subject for Aboriginal art in Australia. They are one of the animal forms assumed by the Aboriginals' 'dreamtime ancestors'. Perhaps it is the physical sustenance given by these ants that inspires humans to portray them in art as nature's helpful ambassadors. A traditional Aboriginal song poem, 'Yurrampi Yilpinji' [Honey-Ant Men's Love Song] from Central Australia represents the travails of a honey ant ancestor in this mode.[25] According to the song's editor, when a group of men sings this song – which by tradition was actually composed by the

Honey ants
are a popular
subject for
Australian
Aboriginal art.
Florie Jones
Napangardi,
*Honey Ant
Dreaming.*

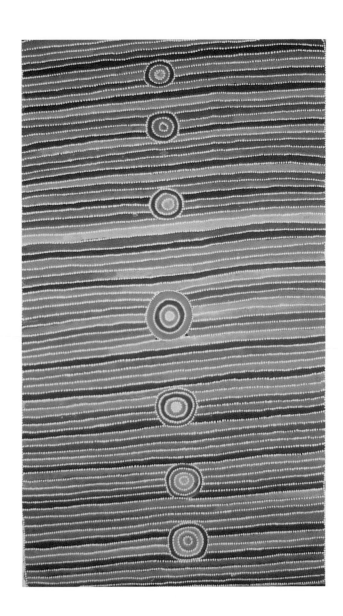

dreamtime ancestor – it has power to attract a certain woman to one of their number. The ant, as both the song's composer and model for the singer's life, is a minion helping him to find love – figurative sweetness.

The song's narrative takes place on a dual time-scale. It is set and composed within the dreamtime framework of the Aborigines' ancestors, yet is performed within and impacts upon the present. The hopeful singer participates in an ancient drama of love shared with the dreamtime ancestors. His present situation shadows and intersects with the narrative of the poem, a kind of Ur-love story whose main character is a dreamtime ancestor named Honey-Ant. So closely are the lives of the singers and ancestor intertwined, however, that the poem's title translates in the plural: the performers are all, in a sense, honey-ant men, at least for the duration of the song. In this sense, it is another creation myth weaving together the characteristics of ants and humans.

In the song, Honey-Ant sets out from home on a long journey, and on his way sees a woman whom he desires. He performs a ceremony to attract the woman, and a Red Bird acts as go-between. When the bird has done its work, Honey-Ant becomes literally like his animal icon (interestingly, in female form like the ant):

Abdomen swollen, Honey-Ant emerged from a hole,
Went well satisfied,
With eggs laid.

With sorrow at leaving her home, the woman follows behind Honey-Ant as he returns to his own place. Along the way she digs, seemingly literally, for ant-food, and metaphorically in search of union with Honey-Ant himself. Eventually the woman comes back to Honey-Ant's country and settles with him. At this point, however, the song becomes very difficult to interpret, and somewhat disturbing. There are suggestions that their initial encounter was one in which she caught *him* like a honey ant and then extracted his honey. Later, 'He asked for honey' but she tells him 'Not enough honey'. The editor comments that the sexual symbolism of honey and its withholding has its parallel in European thought.

At this point, the editor's claim that this is a song sung to attract a woman begins to seem only a partial interpretation, for this does not have the happy ending of a love song. It appears more like another variety of song he describes: one sung as a thoughtful reflection on love and the difficult process of finding it. At first, semi-natural beings in the form of ant ancestors aid Honey-Ant in his search, just as natural signs will lead a competent bushman to a source of sweetness in the desert. These ants do not, however, quite seem to be minions. Initially they are guides and co-participants in the search. Latterly in the poem, as the metaphor shifts and the woman's favour is shown to be elusive like honey and its guardians, 'Yurrampi Yilpinji' may be read as a meditation on humans' inability to control love as easily as Psyche controlled her ant-minions. The desirous man is both hunter and hunted, and the honey ant plays a more ambiguous, complex role than in the Graeco-European tradition.

Though some of Aesop's tales and the case of the honey ants suggest interesting problems for the miniature-army interpretation of ants, there is no doubting the ubiquity of this representation. For many cultures, the fairy-tale triumph of the apparently inferior suggests that ants would indeed make a powerful force for anyone who could control them; their tiny world makes the observer seem safe, and powerful in comparison. The nostalgic aspect of miniaturization can also be seen in ant representations, with their close connections to childhood – even the childhood of humanity itself, through the ancient and contemporary creation myths involving ants. Perhaps these too are an effort to control present existence, through a comforting interiorization of history itself. No wonder Otto Bismarck, when asked how he would choose to be reincarnated, is supposed to have replied as follows:

> If I had to choose the form in which I would rather live again, I think it would be as an Ant. Just see: this little creature lives under a perfect political organization. All Ants are obliged to labour, to lead a useful life; all are industrious, and perfect subordination prevails, with discipline and order.[26]

There is, one suspects, no question about how the Iron Chancellor saw himself in respect to these perfect subordinates. He fantasized about having their army under perfect, ant-like control.

3 Ants as Models

Proceeding from the grand, regal overview of the previous chapter and down into the nest itself, we can see how the behaviour of ants has provided role models for those who observed them.

> Go to the ant, thou sluggard; consider her ways, and be wise:
> Which, having no guide, overseer, or ruler,
> Provideth her meat in the summer, and gathereth her food in the harvest.[1]

These, Solomon's injunctions, are of course the most famous moral assessment of the little six-legged creatures, but the ant's supposed virtues of industry, prudence and mutual aid were extolled by a great number of people. In fact, Solomon's impression of the ant has been repeated in fables by Aesop, La Fontaine and the Disney studio. The moral interpretation of ants has varied considerably: Victorian platitudes, socialist utopias and Nazi eugenics have all been inspired by looking closely at the way ants behave.

AESOP AND HIS RE-INTERPRETERS

As I argued in the previous chapter, it would be hasty to describe Aesop as a moralist in his treatment of the ant. But his most

Ants in a miniature in a bestiary from Peterborough. Medieval bestiaries often linked the ant's acute sense of smell with the Christian's ability to distinguish orthodoxy from heresy.

famous fables about ants do seem to underline Solomon's assessment, and concern their supposed prudence. In one, 'The Ant and the Beetle', the ant has spent its summer busying itself, collecting grain from the fields to store for the winter, exactly as Solomon describes. A dung-beetle, watching all this, expresses astonishment that the ant never rests as the other insects do. When winter comes, however, the beetle's dung-ball, its supply of food, is washed away, and it comes begging for sustenance to the ant. The ant replies that it will not give the beetle any of its store, adding that the beetle should have worked harder during the summer. In a very similar story, 'The Ant and the Grasshopper (or Cicada)', the ants are laying out some of their grain store to dry in the winter, when a hungry grasshopper comes along asking for something to eat. 'I could not gather food like you in summer,' it explains; 'I was busy making music.' The ants laugh, and reply 'since you sang in summer, now you may dance'.

An 1864 illustration of La Fontaine's 'The Cicada and the Ant', by 'Grandville' (Jean Ignace Isidore Gérard).

Jean de La Fontaine retells only the latter of these judgmental fables, doing so with a wonderfully harsh flippancy.[2] Despite the apparent severity of the tale, it would be a mistake to think that La Fontaine was preaching through it. Anyone who has read his scurrilous *Contes et Nouvelles en Vers* will attest that situational irony and *schadenfreude* are the moral phenomena that most interest him. As Guido Waldman has remarked, La Fontaine himself was not on the side of the ant, but was rather 'like the Grasshopper in his famous fable, ... temperamentally incapable

A 1745 illustration of La Fontaine's 'The Cicada and the Ant'.

The Provençal hermit and insect-lover J. H. Fabre hated ants and La Fontaine's fable with a passion. His illustration (1912) of the two creatures shows ants crawling on cicadas, seeking to parasitize their water source.

of prudent management and squander[ing] his fortune rather rapidly, the succession of ladies in his life being the major beneficiaries'.[3] A man like this seems unlikely to have had moralizing in mind when he retold Aesop's fable. Perhaps La Fontaine enjoyed a joke at the expense of the South, through their symbol, the cicada, or even relished its implicit reference to that carefree, wealthy nest – the Versailles court that was his patron.

La Fontaine's contemporary Bernard Mandeville had a similarly libertine attitude. During his time in England, the Dutch polymath satirized the prevalent moral obsession with bees.

Mandeville, too, consciously placed his insects in the tradition of Aesop and his fables, having earlier published *Aesop Dress'd or a Collection of Fables Writ in Familiar Verse* in 1704. In ironic reference to the often-quoted 'happy hum' of their apparently cheerful busyness, Mandeville's poem was originally entitled *The Grumbling Hive*. He later re-wrote it as *The Fable of the Bees, or, Private Vices, Publick Benefits*. From Mandeville's perspective, the bees' commonweal was revealed to be nothing but the combined outcome of personal selfishness and altogether base morals.

In 1998 Disney and Pixar reinterpreted Aesop's tale yet again as *A Bug's Life*. In this version, the honest, hardworking, all-American ants do not laugh at the grasshoppers, for they are a kind of invader/Mafia hybrid, demanding grain with menaces at the end of each summer. (At times, the grasshoppers remind the viewer visually of the dinosaurs in *Jurassic Park*.) The ants finally manage to beat off the grasshoppers with the aid of an outsider flea-circus troupe, reasserting their rights of property over the demands of the parasites. Because the grasshoppers, for all their might, actually need the ants, the ants conclude that they are in fact the superior species, stronger in this sense than the grasshoppers who cannot stand on their own six feet. Towards the end of the film, the princess ant stands up to the grasshopper's leader and tells him 'You see, nature has a certain order. The ants pick the food, the ants *eat* the food, and the grasshoppers *leave*.' Thus the film affirms the American dream: the right to the goods earned by one's own toil. Contemporary US Internet satires on the tale, where the grasshoppers are the IRS (tax office), liberals or Democrats, give a general cultural basis to this interpretation. A counter-cultural interpretation of the same tale is given by the satirical American paper *The Onion*® in its June 2000 issue. Ants 'teach children about toil, death', it proclaims, above a picture of a 'Playscovery Ant Village'.

One editor in 1665 moralized Aesop's 'The Ant and the Fly' thus: 'Short life and merry, give me Ease, this crys, / While that with Sweat and Care his Marrow drys: / These are extremes; upon the Medium fix; / Study, and Toyl, with Recreation mix.'

THE FLY AND THE ANT.

Satirizing moral uses of ant behaviour, *The Onion* ® led in June 2000 with news of the 'Playscovery Cove Ant Village', 'the fun way to teach your kids to accept their miserable fate stoically'.

NATURAL THEOLOGY

One particular trend in Aesopian interpretation is worth highlighting, and concerns the use of insect fables during the late eighteenth and early nineteenth centuries. At this time, many considered that God's word in the Bible was supplemented by the revelations He had laid out all around in the 'book of nature'. The natural world contained moral lessons and illustrations of God's wisdom and love, claimed these writers, if only one would study it carefully enough. Collectively, they created a corpus known as natural theology. Although natural theology had ceased to be at the forefront of natural philosophy by about the 1830s, its products continued well into the nineteenth century. Travel literature from this period, and children's books, even from the twentieth century, all pictured ants in ways that were supposed to inspire emulation. Nature's 'is' communicated God's 'ought'.

In the earlier, more genteel days of natural theology, the Reverend William Gould published a classic of the genre, *An Account of English Ants* (1747). This was his reflection upon the ants, showing clearly the kinds of ways in which nature was read as a divine lesson. It would not be difficult to believe that parts of it had gone into his sermons.

[The ants'] surprising affection towards their young might teach us to value posterity and promote its happiness . . . Their incessant labours may serve to enliven the industrious, and shame the lazy part of mankind. The unanimous care exerted by each colony for the common emolument might let us know the consequence of public good, and tempt us to endeavour the prosperity of our own countrymen. From their economy we may learn prudence; from their sagacity wisdom. If, lastly, we call to mind the infinite curiosities that distinguish a settlement of ants; the form and structure of the common workers; the glorious character of the queen; the strange unparalleled circumstances that attend the flies; the remarkable changes of the young; the different species and particular use they answer in the scale of beings; we cannot but extol the majesty of God, who has arrayed the universe with so much beauty, and embellished each part of it with such a scene of wonders. 'Great is the Lord, and marvellous, worthy to be praised; there is no end of his greatness.'[4]

The Reverend William Kirby, co-writer of *Introduction to Entomology* (1815–26), also used nature as his text, devoting considerable discussion to Solomon's words on ants in Proverbs. It was important for him to prove that European ants also gathered and stored seeds, and not just the harvester ants of the Middle East, whose distinctive behaviour the writer of Proverbs appeared to describe. By doing this, Kirby was able to demonstrate that God, through nature, had provided the same moral lesson for Israelite and European alike; Aesop and the Bible were re-established as authorities applicable to all.

The birth of political economy brought with it a renewed interest in the social insects, despite Mandeville's earlier satire. Bees exemplified economy for a society recently impressed by the philosophy of Adam Smith; they divided their labour to produce profit in the form of honey, which was then stored up for the common good. A writer in this tradition commented:

> . . . the economy of the bee does not simply refer to its disposition to lay up a store of provisions for the support of itself and its young in times of scarcity, but also to the wise and prudent management of its household, by which every member has its appointed duties, to be carried out for the general benefit of the community . . . Those who inhabit the human hive are most happy who understand best the economy we have been speaking of. They study economy of time, of food, of clothes, and of every description of property, and they feel that to waste any of these is sinful . . . Such people are not selfish – it is only shallow thinkers who call them so; they accumulate property, it is true, but with it they increase their means of doing good, for it is obviously those who know the value of property that can lay it out to the best advantage either for themselves or for others.[5]

This emphasis on the economic virtues of social insect was easily blended with the moral recommendations of natural theology. In 1851, the Society for the Promotion of Christian Knowledge (SPCK) published two volumes concerning natural history and animal morals. The whole of the second volume was devoted to insects, with ants forming a major part of it. The anonymous author, echoing Gould's words, recommended that the ant provided an admirable example of prudence to his (or her) readers. This was why Solomon had classed the ant amongst the 'four things which are little upon the earth, but exceeding wise', for though 'The Ants are a People not strong, Yet they provide their food in the summer.'

Within this nineteenth-century context, Aesop's fable acquired a much clearer moral overtone than there had been to Mandeville and La Fontaine's renderings, one hundred and fifty years earlier. There was no doubt that readers of the fable were now supposed to identify with the ant rather than that unsuccessful supplicant, the beetle or grasshopper. But was the fable supposed to discourage indulgence when approached by the

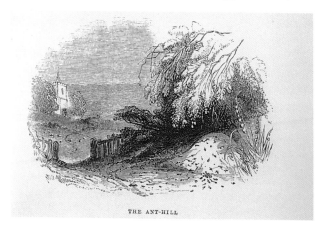

THE ANT-HILL

A rural formic idyll shows a church not far away, reminding readers of ants' many Godly qualities. An illustration from the anonymous *Lessons Derived from the Animal World* (1851).

less fortunate, or was it supposed to warn about the world's lack of mercy upon the unprepared? The SPCK writer was inclined to interpret the winter's effects on insects – bringing plenty or starvation – as God's judgement upon their moral actions during the summer. He (or she) remarked that 'the general course of events plainly shows that it is the good pleasure of the Almighty to bless the industrious and prudent man, and to give him a large share of what the world calls good fortune'.[6] Within the natural theology of a laissez-faire creation, there was a twofold obligation: to provide for oneself, and not to allow charity to obstruct the function of God's economic laws.

An optimistic natural theology of social insects has survived despite the shadows of Darwinian, selectionist philosophy (whether it was God or Nature that did the judging). As late as 1867, George Cruikshank was inspired to make his engraving 'The British Bee Hive'. It showed the layered elements of society – the Forces the Bank, the Trades, the Arts – upholding the upper elements of the hive: the State, Queen Victoria, and her family.

And at the turn of the twenty-first century, there are Christian and Islamic texts that still draw upon the life of the ant in order to explicate the qualities of God. During the writing of this book, an Internet search turned up a number of religious or inspirational tracts based on ants, including a United Church of God sermon based on the preacher's encounter with a Texan ants' nest. In true natural theological tradition he prefaced his remarks: 'that fire ant colony really preached this sermon to me and I am just going to pass it along to you today'. A Muslim site uses the ant colony's 'great and perfect order' to preach 'proof [of] the inspiration of a certain "supervisor,"' and to recommend that the reader likewise should 'put [their] trust in God'.

The details of natural theological interpretation are frequently of interest, revealing as they do norms of society and culture which may not otherwise be visible to the historian.[7] This section opens up one specific area, the domestic, in which natural theologians of the nineteenth century made ant-derived recommendations. The following two sections go into further detail, showing how two particular aspects of the ants' domestic economy were re-interpreted to give moral lessons that fitted in with the moral climate of the day. The first of these accounts concerns workers. Constituting the vast majority of ants inside the colony, these were variously used to recommend a humble obedience towards one's superiors and radical forms of socialism. Secondly, the queen of the colony was used both as a model for monarchy and for maternity.

The domestic economy of the ants was particularly important to the Victorians, who strove to build a private sphere in the home: a place for men to be with their women and children, distinct from the public world of work. Magazines and journals such as Charles Dickens's *Household Words* were produced to cater for this new, self-conscious market. The home was also an important place for the transmission of moral and religious instruction, so ants' existence in a domestic sphere of their own made them an especially appropriate example from nature's theology.

A. S. Byatt has produced, in fictional form, arguably the most perceptive examination of these parallels that Victorians so loved to draw between formic and human domesticity. In her novella *Morpho Eugenia* (1992), an impoverished naturalist, William Adamson, has recently returned from a collecting trip to the Amazon. Having lost his collection, and lacking the

An early depiction
of 'domestic
arrangements: an
anthill, a woodcut
from Ulisse
Aldrovandi's
*De animalibus
insectis . . .*
(Bologna, 1638).

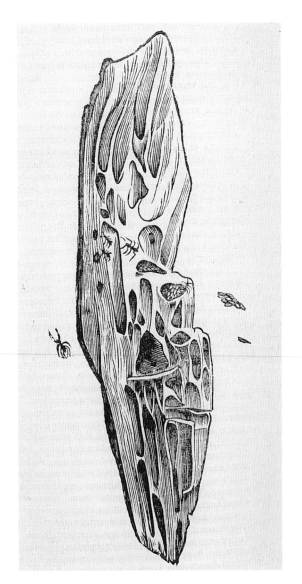

William Adamson shows an artificial formicary to the children of Bredely Hall in *Angels and Insects* (1995).

means to gather another, he accepts employment by a wealthy, upper class patron, the Reverend Harald Alabaster, who wishes him to organize his natural history collection. Adamson is out of his social depth at the Alabasters', all the more so when he falls in love with one of the daughters, Eugenia. Adamson's gradually increasing familiarity with the organization and the mores of the Alabaster household is echoed by a project undertaken by the governess. Together with the children, and under Adamson's guidance, she studies an ant colony in the grounds of Bredely Hall. As the novella progresses, Byatt alerts the reader to ironic comparisons between the two 'households', comparisons which may or may not be apparent to the characters themselves.

With Adamson's advice, the governess is able to capture a queen and create an artificial formicary for the children to observe:

Many of the internal processes of the nest – the Queen's industrious parturition, the workers' perpetual grooming and nourishment of her, their carrying-off and nursing of eggs, their shifting of eggs and larvae to nurseries that were warmer or cooler – could be seen in the glass-sided nest in the schoolroom . . .[8]

In just the same way, Adamson finds himself a strange, mis-proportioned observer of life in his new residence, pampered with material comfort and constricted by social roles – caste roles – entirely new to him:

Understanding life at Bredely Hall was not easy. William found himself at once detached anthropologist and fairy-tale prince trapped by invisible gates and silken bonds in an enchanted castle. Everyone had their place and their way of life, and every day for months he discovered new people whose existence he had not previously suspected, doing tasks of which he had known nothing.[9]

As the novella unfolds, the parallels between humans and insects grow increasingly disturbing. Ultimately, Adamson discovers that even the incestuous impregnation of the nest's new queens is a phenomenon not restricted to the formic house-hold. Throughout the story, Byatt pays remarkable homage to the Victorian obsession with domesticity in the animal king-dom. The degree of her characters' insight into their situation is never overstated, and the story's ending, uncharacteristic of nat-ural theology to say the least, is an intentionally contemporary reassessment of the nineteenth century's moral contradictions in such matters.

Conservative natural theologians of the nineteenth century saw the order of the ants' nest as God's way of teaching a person his or her place within society. The SPCK author praised the humble, diligent labours of the worker ants, and the lesson intended for the reader is quite clear: go thou and do likewise. '[The] duties [of the working ants] would seem too great to be borne by such minute agents; yet they are patiently gone through, by dint of the incessant foraging which we see on every side.' Or, speaking of the new adult bee's assiduity in escaping from the cell in which it had been cocooned, the same author quoted an early nineteenth-century authority: 'It appears to know that it is born for society, and not for selfish pursuits; and, therefore, it invariably devotes itself and its labours to the benefit of the community to which it belongs.'[10] The worker, clearly, should not aspire to anything greater, or easier, but should modestly fulfil his or her allotted role.

In Byatt's *Morpho Eugenia* the industriousness of the worker ants, observed by the governess and Adamson, inevitably reminds the reader of the domestic servants of Bredely Hall, who sustain its life by their invisible labours:

> The servants were always busy, and mostly silent. They whisked away behind their own doors into mysterious areas into which [Adamson] had never penetrated, though he met them at every turning in those places in which his own life was led. They poured his bath, they opened his bed, they served his meals and removed his dishes. They took away his dirty clothes and brought back clean ones. They were as full of urgent purpose as the children of the house were empty of it.[11]

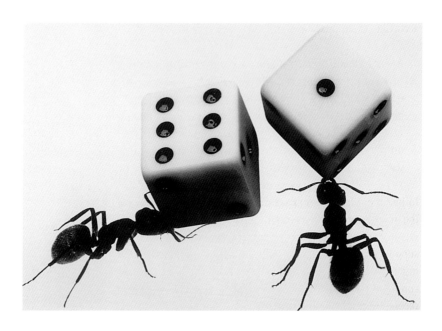

Conceptual image representing the model strength and indefatigability ascribed to worker ants.

The intellectually frustrated governess inscrutably remarks on this conventional moral interpretation:

> 'Maybe they are all perfectly content in their stations', observed Miss Crompton. Her tone was neutral, so extraordinarily neutral that it would have been impossible to tell whether she spoke with irony . . .[12]

Like it or not, in some respects, Victorian British society could seem incredibly similar to the ants'.

Another class-related feature of ant life discussed by Victorian moralists was their kindness to one another or 'mutual aid'. Ants were observed to feed one another, to groom one another, to tend to their wounded companions, and even, according to some, to bury and mourn their dead:

> Among those inhabiting the same colony, there is much
> of what appears to be kindness and goodwill . . . Distress
> or difficulty falling upon any member of their society
> generally excites their sympathy, and they do their
> utmost to relive it . . . When a burden is too heavy for
> one, another will soon come to ease it of part of the
> weight . . .[13]

In just the same way philanthropists encouraged members of
the nineteenth-century working class to set up Mutual or
Friendly Societies for their savings, capital loans, and for their
support in old age. Charles Darwin himself engineered such an
organization for the poor in his Kent village. All this behaviour
could be read into the behaviour of ants and bees; it was
recommended by nature itself.

Such kindness, however, as we have already seen in the case
of the ant and the grasshopper, had a limit. If there were too
much of it, some ants would be encouraged to become dependent, non-contributory members of the nest. They would finish
by draining its resources and making life difficult for their more
deserving and productive compatriots. In this way, the
Victorians made sense of the so-called 'massacre of the drones'.
Male bees, known as drones, were there to perform the function
of 'father of the hive'. Beyond impregnation of the queen, these
'indolent' individuals played no other apparent role in the life of
the nest. In summer, they were observed to be put to death by
the workers. The SPCK writer judged that 'the object of this exter-
mination seems to be to get rid of the idle part of the population, which having no further office to perform in the hive,
would prove a useless burden to the rest of the community'.[14]

The bees' unwillingness to support lazy peers was naturally replicated in the human realm: 'The same [ungenerous] disposition is observed in society towards those who spend all their earnings upon themselves; when they can work no more the honey is given with a grudging hand . . .'.[15] The ants, meanwhile, had a neater solution to the problem of extraneous males. Rather than keep them in the nest, they raised them until the moment of the nuptial flight, at which point they set them free into the high summer air to shift for themselves. In fact none survived long after the 'marriage'; they had no place to go, no role to fit, and most were eaten by birds. It was a perfect, natural out-working of Adam Smith's laissez-faire philosophy.

A little later, socialist writers began to claim that the worker caste in ant life actually conformed to *their* ideals, and that humans should learn a collectivist lesson from their six-legged cousins. The Russian anarchist Peter Kropotkin was one of these. He praised at length the social organization of the ants, and the 'mutual aid' which he perceived amongst them. Kropotkin thought that the degree of mutual aid in a species corresponded to that species' place on the evolutionary scale: the more mutual aid, the higher the animal – with anarchist humans as the peak of evolution. For him, social insects were the highest forms of invertebrate (higher, indeed, than some vertebrates). 'The ants and termites', he judged, 'have renounced their "Hobbesian war," and they are the better for it.'[16]

One of the most important socialist writers on ants was the Swiss psychiatrist and ant enthusiast Auguste Forel (see Chapter 2). In his opinion, the workers were the most important members of the nest, with a truer claim to status than the so-called 'queen'. Forel wrote that 'the ants taught [him] what work was, and the sense of communal life'.[17] This lack of individualism displayed by the ants was something that ought to be emulated by human beings. Forel thought that humans could achieve something like the morally superior society of the ants through education promoting obligatory social work. This work, inspired by ant workers, would bring about the freedom of socialism:

> As a basis for education, [obligatory social work], if well co-ordinated from childhood onwards with the heredi-tary aptitudes of each human being, ceases to be the drudgery nowadays described by our reactionary . . . capitalists . . . Rather does it become . . . so beneficial that the individual can scarcely dispense with it in later years.[18]

One of the key worker behaviours observed by Forel was the process of mutual feeding. His skilled dissections of ants revealed to him that ants have two stomachs: an ordinary one for digestion, and an upper crop where food could be stored for regurgitation to hungry nest-mates. Forel named this organ 'the social stomach', for it was shared by the whole community. A needy ant would approach her companion, waggling her antennae in a friendly manner, and would induce the replete worker to give up some of her stored food. If just one worker were allowed to feed on a sugary solution stained with blue dye, the whole nest-full soon acquired the tell-tale tint, showing just how much the process took place. The balloon-like honey ants (see Chapter 1) were just an extreme version of the mutual-feeding phenomenon, ubiquitous throughout the ant world. Forel was so impressed by this act of sharing that he employed it as the key image to capture his ants' communalist utopia, using it as the frontispiece to his major work, *The Social World*

Forel's utopian, formic emblem: 'Work Conquers All'.

of the Ants Compared with that of Man (French original 1921–2), together with the socialist caption *Labor Omnia Vincit* (Work Conquers All). Forel's psychiatric programme of re-educating social misfits was meant to instil a social brain into them, an organ that would then perform the same function as the stomach of the ants. This was how he understood nature's lesson as revealed in the ant. 'Predatory, egoistic and hypocritical though human nature may be in itself by inheritance, yet it can be tamed from childhood upwards *by social education*. My perception of this I owe in the first place to . . . the study of ants.'[19]

QUEEN OR MOTHER?

The Queen Ant, another contested model from the nest, has a remarkable cultural history. During the eighteenth century, when the bee was the more popular human comparison, the largest inhabitant of the nest was actually considered to be the King Bee.[20] When 'he' was discovered to lay eggs, some time in the seventeenth century, and was renamed a Queen, the same conclusions were applied to ants. Now that the leader was no longer male, however, assumptions about the active nature of his authority began to change. It made less sense to see a female figure as a wielder of power, although the Reverend Gould did still comment favourably upon the 'obedience [subject ants] pay their respective queens'. Scholarship in the wake of the French Revolution further downgraded the role of the Queen.[21]

By the latter part of the nineteenth century, some writers had dispensed with the term 'queen' altogether, finding it an inappropriate term to describe the founding female of the nest. Van Bruyssel, author of *The Population of an Old Pear-Tree* (see Chapter 2) was one of these: in his two chapters on ants, he made no mention at all of a 'queen', only 'females' and 'mothers'.

> In the internal view of an ant commune's affairs the most
> striking facts are the relations of the queen mother. Her
> queenhood is wholly fanciful, except in the first stages of
> her independent career. Her motherhood is the great fact
> of life to her and her fellows. It is as a mother that she is
> the destined foundress of a new community.[22]

Seeing the central figure of the nest as a mother changed the moral overtones of her description.

One aspect of these moral overtones concerned the 'nuptial flight'. Each summer, on a certain day, fertile males and females swarm up into the air to mate. The impregnated females return to earth, shed their wings, and start a nest of their own. Gould was astonished by the process, and in his 1747 book he concluded:

> . . . the casting of their wings . . . are to other insects, their
> highest decorations . . . On the reverse, a large ant-fly
> gains by their loss, and is afterwards promoted to the

throne, and drops these external ornaments as emblems of too much levity for a sovereign.[23]

For writers of the late nineteenth century, the shedding of the wings was a metaphor for a woman's transition into the serious business of motherhood and the abandonment of flirtation.

Our ants have obtained their freedom, and wander joy-fully in space. Does not the young girl at her first ball feel as if she were in ethereal realms of poetry? Does she wish to know what happens to the insect, small though it be, attired like her for the great summer season? . . . Each seeks for one to love, and thus they meet at last in a blaze of light beneath the blue sky, amid the harmony of nature. Then they stop in their rapid flight, shake their wings, and find them useless. Of what further service would they be except to fly from happiness? A bride, a wife, a mother, must dream no longer! such is our ant's opinion![24]

In *Morpho Eugenia*, there is no doubt that Lady Alabaster is the Queen of Bredely Hall. Like the Queen Ant, her job is merely to reproduce. In this case, 'queen' is an utter misnomer, for Lady Alabaster exercises no effectual authority in her 'nest'. As the source of fertility, however, the Queen is the *raison d'être* of the nest, lying at its very heart and endlessly cosseted by workers:

Lady Alabaster spent her days in a small parlour . . . she seemed to spend most of her day drinking – tea, lemon-ade, ratafia, chocolate milk, barley water, herbal infusions, which were endlessly moving along the corri-dors, borne by parlourmaids, on silver trays . . . She was

The queen enjoys her brief moment of gauzy elegance before settling down to motherhood. An illustration from Auguste Forel, *Social World of the Ants Compared with That of Man.*

hugely fat, and did not wear corsets except for special occasions, but lay in a sort of voluminous shiny tea gown, swaddled in cashmere shawls and with a lacy cap tied under her many chines . . . Sometimes Miriam, her personal maid, would sit by her and brush her still lustrous hair for half an hour at a time, holding it in her deft hands, and sweeping the ivory-backed brush rhythmically over and over. Lady Alabaster said that the hair-brushing eased her headaches.

Lady Alabaster even physically resembles the Queen Ant studied by the governess: 'swollen and glossy . . . fragile . . . whitish'.[25]

Around the turn of the twentieth century, the quality of motherhood became an issue of burning importance for Europeans and Americans of European origin. There were fears

Lady Alabaster, queen of the Bredely Hall 'nest', is tended by her servant workers in *Angels and Insects* (1995).

that the race might be degenerating, growing lazy, and slipping backward in evolutionary terms. The English upper-middle class worried that the poor were out-breeding them; white Americans worried that immigrants of other 'races' were doing the same. For these people, salvation lay in responsible mother-hood. In Britain, Marie Stopes encouraged contraception amongst poor women, while family allowance was introduced to produce the opposite result amongst desirable breeding stock. Again, ants provided the model. In the ant colony, repro-duction was rationally controlled, with a division of labour between the fertile mother and the assiduous nurses.

Auguste Forel was again one of the most important writers in this vein. Forel was convinced by his treatment of alcoholics and lunatics that society was in a parlous condition, that parents passed their defects onto their children through heredity and education, and that it was therefore vital that humanity learned some things about maternity from the ants. In acknowledgement of these facts, he named his own family home 'La Fourmilière' (The Ant-Colony) and described his wife, Emma, in terms oddly reminiscent of the ant queen/mother, spreading a nebulous influence for the good of the nest, yet without issuing any actual commands: 'From her quiet, almost imperceptible activities an intelligent kindness was irradiated upon our patients . . . our children, and the whole asylum staff . . . Not without reason was she known as "la petite maman."'[26]

Even a feminist myrmecologist was focused on the notion of maternity among the ants. Adele M. Fielde, a one-time missionary and latter-day convert to science, saw the mother's role as crucial in sustaining the quality of the nest – or family – and the race. The division of labour in the nest, with nurses performing the functions of infant care, also justified her own

Yvorne — La Fourmilière

Auguste Forel's home, *La Fourmilière* (The Ant Colony), c. 1900.

life, spanning the nineteenth and twentieth centuries. Like Forel, she felt that responsible motherhood was the most valuable service that a woman could perform for society. But after her fiancé died, she remained single for her entire life, and had no children. Nevertheless, as she explained in her lectures and writing, she felt that her years were worthwhile; as an educator, she performed that part of a mother's role which, in the ant colony, devolved upon the nurses. In ant terms, she was a vicarious 'mother'.

THE ULTIMATE MODEL

Ant society appeared so perfectly, rationally organized to some writers in the twentieth century – particularly in the area of motherhood – that they concluded ants were practising eugenics. Such writers also tended to assume that this was a lesson humans would do well to learn from nature. The German novelist and travel writer Hans Heinz Ewers published a book on ants in 1925, noting that:

> . . . very severely wounded individuals are seldom nursed; those whose death is imminent are cast out of the nest. Just so the Spartans exposed their sickly or crippled children on rocky Taygetus. It seems to me more humane to give over the hopelessly ill or incurably insane to speedy death, rather than to prolong the agony of their lives as much as possible, as we men do; it is a much sounder sentiment for the general good of the people.[27]

Ewers's subsequent descriptions of ant life sound remarkably like recommendations for healthy Aryan youth: he emphasizes their respect for fresh air – evidenced by the ventilation shafts in their nests, cleanliness, and healthy, manly exercise such as 'boxing matches and wrestling matches'. (Ewers does not specify how many limbs are permitted in the Queensberry rules when applied to six-legged competitors.) Such was the German respect for ant society, it was the only country to protect ants by law, forbidding the collection of 'ant-eggs' (actually ant pupae).[28] The reason for this was that ants were considered to be a beneficial member of the forest community. Forest hygiene, as it was known, was an important area of German science: a kind of ecology that was based upon ideas about the native and proper German habitat. Thus native ants participated in the maintenance of the true German landscape, just as their society provided a model for the organization of the human equivalent. The connection between human and formic eugenics is deeper and darker than this. It was not simply words and metaphors that were applied to both populations, but also methods of control. The entomologist Karl Escherich was responsible for developing gas treatments for termite 'pests', well known as the enemies of ants and destroyers of native German trees. These same techniques, the same gases, were soon used to eradicate what the Nazis termed human 'pests'.[29]

4 The Enemy Without

Since biblical times, invading insect hordes have held a peculiar terror for humankind. Besides their devastating economic impact, there is something uniquely nasty about their inhuman form of attack, their countless number, and their irreducibly mass-nature with no individualization whatsoever; where one is crushed, another ten crawl forward to continue its ravages. For the squeamish, their alien body form perturbs, with its hard parts on the outside and a squishy pulp within.

Towards the end of the nineteenth century, ants ceased to be simple role models, and began to be represented in rather less friendly ways, ways that related them to ancient images of the tormenting horde. For decades, if not centuries, stories had existed relating the invasions of ant armies as exotic curiosities. Now, these stories grew in prominence. Graphic accounts of 'army ants' in Africa and South America revealed them to be merciless invaders, consuming alive all creatures in their path.

THE INSECT MENACE

The Insect Menace was published in 1931 by the splendidly named Leland Ossian Howard. Howard was at the forefront of a new class of scientist in America: the professional entomologist. The professional entomologist applied his (or occasionally her) knowledge to the solution of agricultural problems caused by insect pests. Various interests had contributed to the rise of this profession in the period after the Civil War. Capitalists sought a problem-free cultivation of monoculture cash crops; migrating farmers attempted a westward transfer of European and East Coast crops; the Federal government was concerned to appease far-flung States; ambitious young scientists desired to emulate German research ideals. Together, and not without difficulty and disappointment, these parties negotiated the expert niche of the professional entomologist.[1] Howard's book celebrated the achievements of the first and second generations of entomologists, and evangelized about the continuing importance of the cause.

In this and other books, pamphlets and lectures, Howard urged his audience not to underestimate the threat posed by insects. He, and entomologists like him, had plenty of illustrations and examples to make their case. In particular, they used statistics to try and overwhelm their readers with the sheer mass of insects pitted against them. Locusts, for example, were a severe agricultural pest at the very end of the nineteenth century, afflicting Algeria, Cyprus, South Africa and the US. A swarm that struck Kenya in 1928 was sixty miles long and three miles wide.[2] If it were fifty locusts deep, that would make its

'A monster of the past', used as a visual analogy for the threat posed by insects, jointly the 'monster of the present'. Frontispiece for Howard's The Insect Menace (1931).

The nest of the ant lion, from Auguste Johann Rösel von Rosenhof's *Der monathlich-herausgegebenen Insecten-Belustigung . . .* (Nuremberg, 1746–61).

total number of individuals 500,000,000,000, calculated one entomologist. Or if a pair of houseflies was allowed to breed unchecked for one season, it was estimated that they would produce 5,598,720,000,000 progeny. Interestingly, given the argument that the miniature pleasure of insects is about making the world feel safe, these writers often used enlargements of the insects they described to shock and dismay the viewer.

Howard went so far as to place an image of a dinosaur at the front of *The Insect Menace*. It was entitled 'A monster of the past', and was clearly meant to imply that insects should not be regarded as charming collectors' items, but rather as a collective 'monster of the present' – a gigantic, looming force of nature. 'Ant lions' are a more ancient example of miniature monsters. Intriguingly, these creatures (actually dragonfly larvae) that hide in sand funnels ready to trap unwary insects have been represented by some authors as 'lions' that prey on ants, whilst others have imagined that they are ants with leonine powers of predation.

Were ants part of the 'insect menace' in the early twentieth century? Certainly, their numerical properties (two million and more per nest) linked them with the innumerable threat of other insect families. The army ants described in Chapter 1 would also seem to have fitted the bill. Operating in marauding bands, they scoured the landscape and human dwellings for any animal matter, which they consumed utterly before moving on. Yet these actions were not necessarily perceived as frightening. The writer

opposite page: Massed locusts are a potent symbol of the 'insect menace', as in this 1870 engraving.

Army ants (here *Leptogenys processionalis* gp.) display nomadic behaviour, carrying their pupae from place to place as they travel.

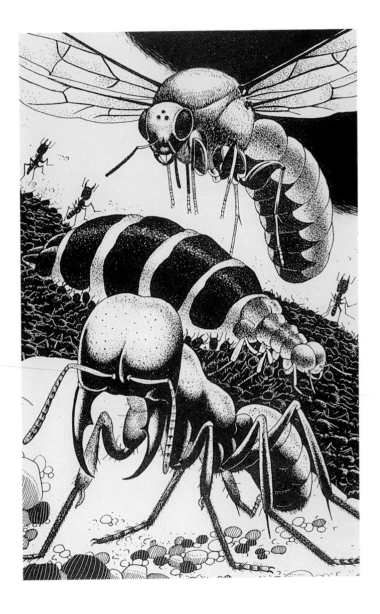

of the natural theology book, *Lessons From the Animal World*, declared '[the ants'] office in nature seems to be to clear off dead and decaying substances, which might otherwise prove offensive, and this is of immense importance to health, especially in warm climates'.[3] A story reported by a Mrs Carmichael of Trinidad followed, relating how a visit by the '*Chasseur ants*' had conveniently rid her house of 'vermin of every kind' whilst she was seated one morning with her family at breakfast. In the twentieth century, the German entomologist Karl Escherich proposed harnessing such to protect tropical plantations by cleansing them of their animal pests.[4]

Siafu ants, a source of terror to European explorers and scientists. The different castes, shown to relative scale, include a large winged male, large queen, and three different castes of worker with their sharp mandibles.

On the whole, however, later explorers and colonists lacked Mrs Carmichael's insouciance. T. S. Savage was a medical missionary from North America who travelled to Africa. Here, he became fascinated by the local wildlife and published a number of papers on it, including two about ants. What amazed him most about ants was their organized method of hunting. They clustered together, before marching out in a vast horde to kill wild animals and livestock. Even ordinarily frightening creatures fell prey to their tiny horror: together they would attack a python when it was gorged and sluggish, cutting it entirely to pieces. The python's mighty coils were of no use against its miniature enemies.

In 1863, the British naturalist H. W. Bates found species with similar habits in South America. 'All soft-bodied and inactive insects fall an easy prey to them', he noted; 'they tear their victims in pieces for facility of carriage'.[5] Thomas Belt, travelling from Britain to Nicaragua on geological surveying business, discovered something that the Nicaraguans called 'army ants'. Belt's 1874 account communicates the military organization shared by all species of the genus and their deadly efficiency.[6] In 1905 a German named J. Vosseler described a terrible race

opposite page: Driver ants depicted in 1954 in terrifying form as they march. Winged male (top), queen (centre), soldier (below) and workers.

Soldier army ant (*Echiton* sp.) with long, sickle-shaped jaws. Some South American peoples use these to suture wounds.

of ant, named 'Siafu' by the local West African people.[7] In the early 1930s the American myrmecologist William Mann found a poisonous stinging ant in Bolivia with 'a length of more than an inch and [an] antagonistic disposition more than worthy of [its] bulk'. This species, known locally as 'buni', would sometimes 'actually drive the bare-footed natives from their own corn patches'.[8] In Brazil, there lived the floridly named *Dinoponera grandis* or 'great terrible ant', known to the locals as the 'tucandero'.

Hans Heinz Ewers, the apparent advocate of ant eugenics, had plenty to say about the hunting ants, so much so that they caused him to rewrite the accepted system of classification for his lay-audience. He named five ant groups descriptively. Four of these referred to innocuous characteristics, such as the 'Long-necked Ants', but the fifth family he named 'Stinging, or Wicked Ants'. Ewers' translator was moved to describe the German's study of ants in purely confrontational terms: 'He has fought the Fire Ants of Texas . . . faced the Wandering Ants in Mexico, and been bitten by the Bull Dog Ants in Australia.'

'Wherever the Ant army goes', wrote Ewers, perhaps thinking of the time one went up his trousers in Australia, 'it spreads terror.'[9]

Ewers had had a particularly unpleasant experience with 'Gypsy Ants' in Mexico. Drunk on the local pulque liquor, and dreaming of a 'Singsong girl [he] had met in Hankow', he had sat down to write her a sonnet although she 'certainly would not understand a word of it'. Happily for the modern reader, Ewers' imperialist fantasies were interrupted by a 'dim peeping' sound. He jumped up, and saw a black, moving carpet on the floor. The peeping sound, he eventually realized, came from behind the cupboard, which concealed 'a Mouse-hole and a Mouse-nest in which lived Mamma Mouse and her Mouse children [who had often squeaked as if to say] "Bring us something good to eat!"' Ewers offered a peculiarly nasty description of what happened next:

> She was a nice, lovely House-mamma. Now she was being eaten up alive, she and her naked Mouse-children . . . If only those Mice were dead at last, thought I, but they squeaked, and squeaked, ever more wildly, uncannily, hopelessly . . .[10]

Mrs Carmichael, made of sterner stuff from a bygone age, would doubtless have poured another cup of tea and told Ewers to think about the health benefits of eliminating murine infestations. Next, the ants turned on Ewers himself. As they 'swarmed . . . and poured' towards him, he managed to step into a large pitcher of water where he remained all night, swaying slightly, until the ants had gone. Other authors also recommended this as a last resort for avoiding ants; a common preventative measure was to stand the legs of one's bed in containers of vinegar or petroleum before retiring.

One of Ewers' contemporaries speculated in graphic terms about what it would feel like to be Mamma Mouse:

> To be bitten to death by the Siafu must be one of the most cruel torments that can be imagined . . . by preference these ants will first attack the delicate mucous portions of the eyes, nose, etc., and they always discover almost at once the most sensitive parts of the skin. Their bite is rendered all the more painful by their instinct for moving their sharp toothed mandibles in the sore.[11]

According to Vosseler, victims could still die of their wounds even if rescued: 'I believe that the Siafu lick the blood of their victims when they cannot immediately tear them to pieces. When the haemorrhage is too violent, or the bitten surface of the skin too large, the victim can no longer be saved.'[12]

The final insult was that the army ants did not stop at displacing people from their homes. They found human roadways and paths ideal for their own rapacious journeys. Both Vosseler and Savage noted the frequency of this phenomenon, which forced people to stay off their own routes.

Despite all this, ants were not *necessarily* represented as part of the 'insect menace'. Ants were not economically important insects. Though their actions were sometimes horrible, they did not destroy crops or eat more than the occasional larder-full of provisions. Yet their threat was exaggerated out of all proportion. For culturally contingent reasons, they were identified with the economically significant hordes battled by Howard and his colleagues.

The reason why army ants were perceived as threatening lies in their location: the colonies. Here they were lumped in with the other insects that bit and pestered the colonists, destroying their crops, depleting their workforce and bringing disease. Most interestingly, their alien quality of danger lay in their supposed kinship with their 'savage' human compatriots.

Various characteristics of army ants revealed that they were an inferior, savage sort of ant. For one thing, their stings related them to wasps, the primitive ancestors of ants. For another, this family of ants did not display the mutual feeding that so impressed Forel in Chapter 3. Moreover they were purely carnivorous, and cared indifferently for their young. The larvae spun a cocoon from which they were left unaided to escape. In the case of failure to do so, they died, and were flung out onto the rubbish heap. They were less fully socialized, less altruistic: altogether less advanced. Army ants were not found in Europe, and contrasted with the more 'civilized' ants found in the old world. European ants were homely, not nomadic; they were fully socialized; they were often vegetarian – some even practising 'agriculture' or 'farming' with aphids. A Victorian liberal politician, John Lubbock (later Lord Avebury) had explicitly compared stages of human social 'progress' with the ants'. Rising up the evolutionary scale, ants, like humans, had passed from hunting to the agrarian and finally the pastoral phase.

All of this figured with the persistent cultural assumption that peaceableness was the mark of the more 'highly evolved' race or culture. What savages settled by blows, gentlemen, and above all ladies, settled by compromise and forbearance. Exotic ants, the Siafu of West Africa, for example, therefore seemed to display a curious kinship with their human counterparts. Forel wrote:

> [I]f certain negroes wish to be revenged on an enemy, they will bury him up to his neck . . . in order to have the savage pleasure of seeing him bitten by a Siafu and killed by inches as they gnaw his head . . . In view of the mentality of the negroes and of the Anomma [genus of ant including the Siafu species], it is even quite probable.[13]

It was as though the troublesome insects were aiding their compatriots in order to defend the continent of Africa against the colonists. In 1909, the British Secretary of State for the Colonies received a memo stating clearly:

> It is not too much to say that the cause of the almost complete closure of Africa – lying as it does at the very foot of Europe – until quite recent times . . . has been the existence of disease- and death-carrying insects and ticks.[14]

Again, this is an interesting image of scale. The whole of Africa – human and insect alike – is miniaturized and placed at Europe's foot, but in this case the shrinkage of the enemy provides no comfort. Instead one is reminded of Achilles' heel. Sitting out his time in India that same year, the Chief Entomologist of the Imperial Department of Agriculture entertained similarly disturbing notions: '[A] combination of the red ants could probably drive human beings out of India . . . and human methods of warfare would require to be revolutionized to deal with it.'[15]

The Europeans' fears about the complicity of savage insects and humans was part of a larger anxiety about degeneration.

H. G. Wells's heroes find the ant-like Selenites in *First Men in the Moon* (1901): "'Insects,' murmured Cavor, "Insects!"'

This has been well documented by historians; predictions that the sun was going to die, that the comforts of civilization would cause evolution to run backwards, that the working classes were out-breeding the rest, and that the white man could not survive the tropics all contributed to the sense that things were going downhill around the turn of the twentieth century.

H. G. Wells, at his peak during this period, was mildly obsessed by the threat of ant-like creatures, and used them to

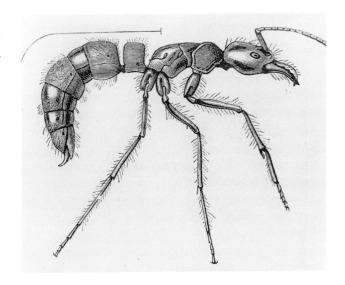

Dinoponera grandis, illustrated here in worker form in 1899, may well be the species on which H. G. Wells based *Empire of the Ants* (1905). Their actual length is about 26 mm.

personify contemporary threats of degeneration. Patrick Parrinder has noted how Wells's monsters are nothing like the little green men we most frequently associate with science fiction.[16] Instead, he has crustacean-like and insectan creatures come to menace humanity: giant crabs infest the dying world's shores in *The Time Machine*, arthropodal aliens stalk the earth in *War of the Worlds*, and the Selenites in *First Men in the Moon* are very clearly modelled on ants. But it is in the short story 'Empire of the Ants' that Wells explores the most topical, degenerative fears about the insect form.

The story centres on an English engineer, Holroyd, who is taken onboard a Portuguese ship whose mission is to investigate reports that giant ants are laying waste to a colony in South America. Although they are large as ants go, they are still too small to be shot, and little enough to swarm and surge like Ewers' black carpet. The ants also seem to have evolved greater

An illustration from H. G. Wells's *Empire of the Ants* (1905), showing a dispute about boarding an ant-infested ship.

intelligence than normal. The Portuguese captain turns out to be incompetent; he sends the lieutenant to his death on an infested ship of human corpses. He futilely fires his cannon at the ants' ranks – ranks that simply scatter and recondense like so many droplets of black water. No wonder, then, that the mission fails. The ship turns around and sails away with all haste, leaving the ants to their new-found mastery of the continent.

What gives the story its bite is its title. The tale goes beyond the fantastic and taps into contemporary fears about the tenability of European empires. Whom did these lands belong to, so far from London, Paris, Madrid? 'In a few miles of this forest there must be more ants than there are men in the whole world!' pondered Holroyd . . .

> In a few thousand years men had emerged from barbarism to a stage of civilization that made them feel lords of the future and masters of the earth! But what was to prevent the ants evolving also? . . . Suppose presently the ants began to . . . use weapons, form great empires, sustain a planned and organized war?[17]

The Boer Wars had shown that the cultures threatening nasty surprises were not formic but human. Suppose the colonized organized themselves for resistance, in ways that had not previously been thought capable? Suppose that the hostile landscape were to throw off its colonists by the collective power of all its natives, both human and animal? Suddenly it was the colonists themselves who appeared tiny and ant-like to Holroyd.

Wells could not resist pushing anxieties about the limits of progress and the fragility of European superiority to their furthest extreme. The narrator, to whom Holroyd has told his story, concludes:

> And why should [the ants] stop at tropical South America? By 1911 or thereabouts, if they go on as they are going, they ought to strike the Capuarana Extension Railway, and force themselves on the attention of the European capitalist. By 1920 they will be half-way down

A movie poster for the film *Empire of the Ants* (1977). Very loosely based on H. G. Wells's story, the film features Joan Collins as an unscrupulous real estate saleswoman and giant ants mutated by toxic waste.

the Amazon. I fix 1950 or '60 at the latest for the discovery of Europe.[18]

ENEMIES ON THE BATTLEFIELD

The horror of Wells's innumerable ants has remained with us,
though not always in its colonial form. The commonly known
fact that ants engage in warfare has given them a particular
edginess in times of human conflict. Like the Secretary of State
with his image of African insects at the foot of Europe, many
combatants have found that the miniature vision of the insect
world was not a comforting interiorization but rather an
unpleasant revelation of the details of war. During the First
World War, the sight of insect-infested corpses made ants a
synecdochic representation of all the forces that threatened to
destroy. Coming upon a dead German, the narrator of Hugh
Walpole's *The Dark Forest* noticed 'Its face was a grinning skull
and little black animals like ants were climbing in and out of the
mouth and the eye-sockets.'[19]

A soldier of the Second World War, engaged in a disastrous
campaign in Italy and under heavy shelling, found the sight of
ants fighting a depressing reminder of the Hobbesian war of all
against all:

In the lulls between explosions I could hear a lark singing.
That made the war seem sillier than ever. I was thinking
how man always mucked up nature when I saw two ants
on a ledge in my trench. The bigger had the other between
its claws, and was dragging it along the ledge . . . the small
ant sprang to life and established a stranglehold of its own
. . . The pattern of attack and counter-attack repeated
itself, the small ant regaining less and less ground. At the

104

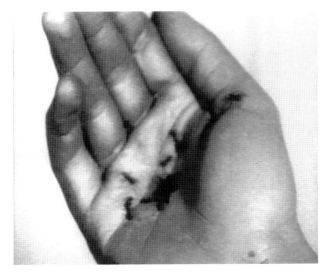

end of one drag it lay motionless . . . I decided that a long-range artillery duel had its points.[20]

Spike Milligan's reminiscences of the Second World War also reveal that ants had somehow impressed their presence upon him during his military service. He recounts a conversation conducted while watching ants dealing with a casualty of their own:

I watched some ants moving a dead grasshopper – 'What you doing?' says Edgington with a tea mug welded to his right hand.
'Watching ants.'
'I wonder what killed him,' said Edge, now squatting.
'It would be his heart.'
'We'll have to wait for the autopsy.'

In Marcantonio Raimondi's *Dream of Raphael* (c. 1507–8) the phallic ant approaching the nude figures may also be a symbol of decay. According to Artemidorus' handbook on the interpretation of dreams (translated and published in Venice in 1518), winged ants are evil omens (ants, 'if they crawl around the body . . . herald death, because they are sons of the earth, and cold and black').

'That might be too late, with his heart an autopsy could kill him.'

I angered a bull ant with a twig.

'Don't let him get hold of it mate,' says Edge, 'or he'll beat the shit out of you.'[21]

In their boredom, Milligan's troops figure the ants as their enemy. In making their enemy tiny, they attempt to manage their fears like the young Forel, but in this case they only succeed in underlining what to them seems like the ridiculousness of the entire conflict. Just as much as the more unpleasant impressions of the other combatants described here, the surrealism of Milligan's imagery recalls Dalí's ants, those unnerving symbols of decay that climb over his melting clock faces and other figures.

Meanwhile, the author T. H. White was busy reducing the threat of fascism to an ant-sized one as he composed *The Book of Merlyn* in 1940. Lying bored and ill in bed, with a toy ants' nest as his only amusement, the young King Arthur begs Merlyn to turn him into an ant (as he has previously enabled him to enter other animal lives). Merlyn warns against the venture, explaining 'They are dangerous . . . The ants are not our Norman ones, dear boy. They come from the Afric shore. They are belligerent.'[22] This colonial imagery soon gives way to more contemporary anxieties, however, for the ants turn out to be subjects of a totalitarian state, terrifying in their mindless obedience. 'EVERYTHING NOT FORBIDDEN IS COMPULSORY' proclaims the notice over each entry tunnel to the nest. The ants' mindless, organized belligerence is soon turned on Arthur, who has to be rescued and restored to his right size.

More recently, Bernard Werber's unusual thriller, also titled

T. H. White's totalitarian ants portrayed by Trevor Stubley in *The Book of Merlyn* (1977), which White wrote during World War Two as the planned conclusion to *The Once and Future King.*

Empire of the Ants, paid homage to Wells's story. The jacket write-up aimed to attract its readers with the creepy announcement, drawn from the novel, that 'during the few seconds it takes you to read this sentence, some 700 million ants will be born on earth'. There is even a word for the goose-pimply sensation 'as of ants crawling over the skin': formication.[23]

RETHINKING COLONIAL IMAGERY

In recent years, as the legacy of colonialism and post-colonialism has been dissected, some people have begun rethinking the colonial origin for images of the ant menace. Christopher Hope, Yukinori Yanagi and Derek Walcott have all sought to redeem such metaphors, subverting them in the first two instances, and recapturing positive aspects of ant life in the other.

Christopher Hope, a white author born in Johannesburg, has written a satire, *Darkest England* (1996), which reverses the 'heroic' journeys of the Victorian explorers into Africa by recounting the journeys of David Mungo Booi, an indigenous South African nomad of the Karoo. Educated by a farmer of English origin, Booi is sent by his people in the 1990s to seek the help of the present Queen (descendant of 'Old Auntie with Diamonds in Her Hair') in once more 'kick[ing] the Boer to Kingdom Come'. All the crassest nineteenth-century misconceptions of Africa are parodied in Booi's naïvely acute understanding of England, while the British have advanced remarkably little in their reactions to the unfamiliarity of Booi's people.

Booi describes his kind by saying 'We are a little people', a phrase which recalls Solomon's classification of the ants amongst those 'things which are little upon the earth, but exceeding wise'.[24] Visitors to Booi's land described his tribe like insects, as 'vermin . . . fleas'. But Hope subverts the colonialists' image of natives as ants in two related ways. First, throughout the novel, Booi is described as an ant bear (aardvark). Used to hunting ants and their eggs, Booi commences to eat the English variety when detained upon his arrival. He finds them 'a little saltier than our Bushman's rice but tolerable if eaten fresh'.[25] Booi continues to harvest his favourite food in garden of an ex-bishop who takes him in, even feeding there upon a swarm of flying ants before an astonished crowd.

Hope's second subversion is that the English and Boers are consistently figured as ants. Booi recollects:

In the next few weeks I discovered that to live in England requires a kind of resolution that people from older, freer cultures know little about. It is as if a man had to spend his life buried up to his neck in an ant-heap. The sky is lowered like a roof . . . But fortunately, being accustomed to nothing better, they have adapted to conditions which would destroy people accustomed to freedom, light and air . . . The natives are less occupants than infestations . . . There is hardly a place on the island they have not colonized, and what they call 'remote places' are to us as crowded as a termites' nest . . .[26]

All in all, the natural scale of things has been reversed. Booi concludes the English have 'an excessively shrunken world view . . . yet paradoxically what is closest to them they consider very large indeed'. Thus 'although the island [England], by our standards, is pitifully small, they talk about it as if it were twice the size of Africa'.[27] Booi the ant bear finds himself staring into a Carrollesque ant-world where the ants imagine themselves to be giants. (Booi attributes their shrunken worldview to the incessant rain, 'excessive moisture . . . shrinking the world to the size of a miniature toy'.) The English and Boer are for him a 'pallid infestation', just as the ants were a symbol of incomprehensible native danger to the colonizing whites.

But something is still not right. Booi the aardvark is repeatedly mistreated and captured, 'trussed like the ant bear', by the people who seem like ants. It is a source of puzzlement and unhappiness to Booi that the normal roles are reversed, and that the ant bear finds himself at the mercy of his natural prey. Booi's conclusion is he has somehow fallen among ant-people whose harmless appearance 'no more noxious than flying ants, no more alarming than the white ants' eggs' is entirely deceptive.[28] Now the ant becomes a metaphor of foreign discomfort, just as it was for the colonists of Africa.

Yukinori Yanagi's 1996 mixed-media installation *Pacific*, like his *World Flag Ant Farm*, consists of ants tunnelling through coloured sand flags, smearing them unrecognizably as they create their alternate colonies.

The artist Yukinori Yanagi has deftly satirized colonialist and nationalist ideologies in his installation *World Flag Ant Farm*. The piece is a chequerboard of sand dyed in the patterns and colours of flags from around the world. Through this he has allowed ants to burrow, their tiny colony cutting right across and through these hard-won symbols of national identity. Looking at the piece, one is reminded that the human urge to expand and protect one's borders is no different to the ants'. Moreover, one realizes, our borders are invisible to them. Ironically, despite our relative scale, it is we who are beneath the perceptual threshold of the ant, and not the other way around. The ant burrows and spreads across a globe in which humans are too insignificant to appear in its gaze.

Derek Walcott's *Omeros* (1990) is a magnificent, epic poem, reclaiming Caribbean history from its colonial chroniclers. Its title is the Greek rendition of Homer, and in this sense recalls the fantasy of controlling the ant army, the Myrmidons encountered in Chapter 2. Walcott's Achille is a fisherman, Helen a waitress tired of the attentions of the male tourists: 'The name, with its historic hallucination,/ brightened the beach . . ./ twinkling from myrmidon to myrmidon, from one/ sprawled tourist to another.'[29] An Irish woman, married to an English owner of a pig-farm and long-settled in the Caribbean, reflects on the infestations of island life, concluding that there are worse kinds than the native:

There was a lot in the island that Maud hated:
the moisture rotting their library; that was the worst.
It seeped through the shawled piano and created

havoc with the felt hammers, so the tuner cost
a regular fortune. After that, the cluttered light

on the choked market steps; insects of any kind,

especially rain-flies; a small, riddling termite
that cored houses into shells and left windows blind;
barefoot Americans strolling into the banks –

there was a plague of them now, worse than the insects
who, at least, were natives . . .[30]

So far, this is in line with Christopher Hope's counter-inter-
pretation of the invading-ant metaphor. But sometimes Walcott
represents oppressed people as ants, doing so with pained pity.
An image of chained men recurs through the poem: prisoners
and slaves. From a distance they often appear to the poet's eye as
ants – not the terrifying marauders of the colonialists' experience, but small creatures, the *fourmis rouges* afraid of water yet
marched en masse to the ocean's edge and on to the pathetic
terror of exile.[31] Towards the end of the book, the authorial voice
comes through relatively directly, as Walcott meditates upon his
own experience of writing *Omeros*. He weighs up the apparent
insignificance of his words against the power and value of
personal history, '. . . strong as self-healing coral, a quiet culture/
. . . branching from the white ribs of each ancestor'. Faced with
the doubt that he is adding mere footnotes to history, Walcott
again reaches for the image of the ant to justify his labours:

My light was clear. It defined the fallen schism
of a starfish, its asterisk printed on sand,
its homage to Omeros my exorcism.
I was an ant on the forehead of an atlas,
the stroke of one spidery palm on a cloud's page,
an asterisk only . . .[32]

Although *Omeros* is in part a poem about the permanence of wounds, there is partial healing to be found in those miniature, interior, ant-like experiences: those personal histories, even though they may appear to others as mere asterisked footnotes on the books of history. Indeed, Walcott recovers and re-names the anonymity of micro-history through his magnification, the formic to the human.

An illustration of this process, one of the poem's set pieces, describes how ants help Old Ma Kilman, proprietor of the No Pain Café, to heal Philoctete. Philoctete is another fisherman, Achille's friend and his competitor for Helen. He has an old sore caused by the gouge of a rusty anchor – simultaneously a bodily memory of his ancestors' ankle chains – which sometimes 'used to burn/ [him] till he bawl'.[33] Ma Kilman enters into communion with the earth, praying to nature to heal Philoctete. The ants are her priests. Immediately she enters the dark wood and removes her hat and wig the ants begin running through her hair, itself 'sprung free as moss', connecting her with the earth. And now the ants provide her incantations:

> . . . as her lips moved with the ants, her mossed skull heard
>
> the ants talking the language of her great-grandmother,
> the gossip of a distant market, and she understood,
> the way we follow our thoughts without any language,
>
> why the ants sent her this message to come to the wood
> where the wound of the flower, its gangrene, its rage
> festering for centuries, reeked with corrupted blood . . .

Where the ants had frightened colonialists with their foreign incomprehensibility, they now whisper to the old woman in

forgotten yet familiar words of healing, buried deeper in memory than the improvised patois by which the present-day islanders communicate. Indeed, it is in retrospect the church preacher who now appears incomprehensible to Ma Kilman, 'making desperate signs . . ./ the deaf-mute anger/ of [an] insect signing a language that was not hers'. And so Ma Kilman 'pray[s]/ in the language of the ants and her grandmother' until Philoctete feels the pain draining away from his sore.[34]

In this episode Walcott redeems the colonial imagery of ants shared by Wells, Vosseler, Forel, Ewers and the like. What he has in common with these earlier writers is the sense that ants are fully identified with the landscape, and with its rooted human inhabitants. For Wells and his ilk, this made ants a threat; like their human compatriots they were innumerable, indistinguishable, and alien in their psychology. But Yanagi's playful suggestion that ants respect no national boundaries is a source of strength for Walcott. Ants may be unremarked stowaways on the slavers' ships, setting up colonies in new lands, forever preserving their familiar ways and reminding the slaves' descendants of home. Or perhaps ants form an international sisterhood married to the land, reminding humans of their links with a landscape *somewhere* in the world, irrespective of oppressors' maps. Either way, their miniature existence enables that interiorization of history Susan Stewart describes in *On Longing*: the personal memory that for Walcott brings healing and affirmation.

Opposite: Like Walcott's ants, Kim Stringfellow's ants act as agents of transformation in her 1991 photographic construction *Transformation of Ceres into a Madonna*. The ants, an attribute of Ceres, signify a connection with the earth where ants burrow and the underground rituals for the Goddess took place.© Kim Stringfellow 2003.

5 The Enemy Within

One of the commonest questions faced by the myrmecologist E. O. Wilson is 'What should I do about the ants in my kitchen?' He likes to reply that homeowners should watch where they step, adding that they should also put down food for the visitors (apparently they are particularly fond of tuna and whipped cream). Wilson's answer is startling because most of us find some primitive horror awoken by the sight of streams of ants heading in and out of our cupboards, from apparently invisible cracks in the floor, walls or doorframe. Most of us immediately give way to a powerful urge to annihilate these flagrant intruders.

Notwithstanding the subversive work of writers and artists like Hope, Yanagi and Walcott, ants continued to be regarded as a threat, requiring destruction, well into the twentieth century. But now the threat was not so much one from the colonies, as one rather closer to home. Even the ants in the kitchen seemed to offer disturbing metaphors for certain aspects of supposedly 'civilized' humanity. Psychiatrists, psychologists and sociologists have all been perturbed by certain aspects of ant life, such as their willingness to tolerate parasites, their unthinking crowd-like behaviour and aggression. At the turn of the twenty-first century, ants' border transgressions have piqued the concern of xenophobes and nationalists. In

„Wollen sie jetzt die Ameisen loswerden oder nicht?"

their different ways, all these phenomena have seemed to indicate that there are forces amongst the ants analogous to those threatening to consume human society from within.

SLAVE-MAKING ANTS AND DEGENERATION

To humans of the nineteenth century, one of the most interesting features of ant life was slavery. Slavery was obviously a question of paramount importance in North America, but it was also a topical issue for the Europeans, who were effectively creating an enslaved workforce in their colonies. In the earlier part of the nineteenth century, ant slavery had shown how supremacy was a natural part of the animal kingdom; towards its end, as degeneration became an abiding concern, it gave a warning about dependency and its consequences.

Thomas Belt was a geologist and engineer by trade, but when he went on a surveying expedition to Nicaragua on behalf of the Chontales Mining Company, it was the ants that grabbed his attention. He wrote up his observations in *A Naturalist in Nicaragua*, published in 1874. Belt's book is often a comparison between Englishmen and the inhabitants of Nicaragua, with ants as the central figures that highlight each contrast. Ants,

An array of products is available to help rid the home of ant invasions. But still the ants keep coming.

'You really want to get rid of those ants now, don't you?' reads this German cartoon, highlighting the disproportionate fury with which we react to ants' infractions into our homes.

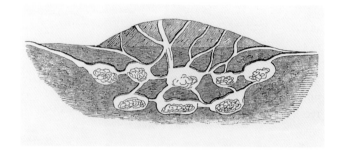

Thomas Belt's approval of the Nicaraguan ants' industry inspired him to draw a cross-section of their nest construction, just as elsewhere in his 1874 book he drew cross-sections of mines.

though adapted to the Nicaraguan landscape, were strikingly like Belt's ideal of Englishmen, while the Hispanic-Nicaraguan people were the very opposite, being lazy, undisciplined and lacking in innovation.

Belt gives many instances of the resourcefulness of ants. In one account some ants, repeatedly crushed by wagons as they crossed a tramway, burrowed underneath the track.[1] By contrast, Belt noted, the locals could not be bothered to build. One Don Filiberto proudly showed him his 'new residence'; Belt was unsurprised to discover this new building consisted of nothing more than four old posts in the ground (which had evidently been there for years) and a smug sense of anticipation.[2] A similar contrast applied to the choice of domestic location. When Belt attacked an ants' nest with carbolic acid, the survivors carefully transported all its contents to a new site. By contrast, the mestizo 'half-breeds' persisted in inhabiting their ancestral homes, even though the edge of the forest had retreated by several miles over the generations, thus necessitating a daily journey of several miles to their plantation and back.[3] In another instance of disparity, leaf cutting ants were scrupulously careful to preserve their leaves in exactly the right conditions, allowing them neither to become too wet nor too dry. Thus, Belt was astonished to discover, they farmed fungus on the leaves, which provided them with a constant source of sustenance. The Victorian reader could not help but think of this when they read that in the village of Muy-muy, 'the land . . . was fertile, but the people too lazy to cultivate it'. Perceiving a 'most depressing aspect of poverty and idleness', Belt asked one man what the people worked at. "Nada, nada, señor," Belt records him as replying; "Nothing, nothing, sir."[4] If only he would go to the ant.

Ever the natural historian, Belt went to work constructing a naturalistic explanation for the comparative inferiority of the Nicaraguans. He concluded that there were two chief factors; the most important was that the mestizo Hispanic-Nicaraguans had been encouraged by the warmth and the land's fertility to become lazy. In addition, the Spanish immigrants had become dependent upon their native workers. By a remarkable coincidence, exactly the same evolutionary process could be discerned amongst the ants.[5] Ants were well known for their slave-making raids – Belt himself recorded one in his book. But what looked like courageous – if amoral – exploitation in the short term turned to long-term disadvantage for the slave-making race. Eventually, over the course of evolution, the pirate ants came to rely on their slaves. They could no longer look after themselves. Some had even degenerated to the condition of having no worker caste of their own. H. G. Wells took the notion to its extreme in his fin-de-siècle *The Time Machine*. In this story, the effete Eloi lived a life of fanciful pleasure; the subterranean Morlocks were responsible for sustaining them, but also preyed upon them. The Eloi were no longer capable of defending themselves against their slaves, now turned predators.

Ants therefore suggested that it was damaging for Europeans to rely on their colonial subjects. In another of Belt's intratextual correspondences, the slave-making raid of some

Ecitons, in which they carry off only the young of their victims, resonates some ten pages later with his account of Nicaraguan settlers. India-rubber prospectors, Belt noted, seized the children of the native Indians whenever they could, under the excuse that they could be baptized as Christians. The authorities, he was sorry to say, 'connived at . . . this shameful treatment'. The implication was that the settlers could hardly be expected to prosper in the long-term if they rested on the labours of others:

> Thinking over the cause of the degeneracy of the Spaniards and Indians, I am led to believe that in climes where man has to battle with nature for his food, not to receive it from her hands as a gift; where he is a worker, and not an idler; . . . there only is that selection at work that keeps the human race advancing, and prevents it retrograding . . .[6]

Such fears applied closer to home, as Wells's Eloi suggested. Was there not a danger that the upper classes, who could afford to have others support them, might also degenerate? A. S. Byatt explores the theme of class and parasitism brilliantly in *Morpho Eugenia* (see Chapter 3). Various members of the Alabaster family, supported by their scuttling army of workers, reveal themselves to be inbred, physically effete and mentally inadequate. The naturalist employed by Lord Alabaster and the frustrated, intelligent, governess Miss Crompton can hardly help but remark the contrast. Observing some slave-making ants, the naturalist offers some apparently dispassionate information for the governess's illumination:

Mr Darwin observes that when these British Blood-red

Ants migrate, they carry their slaves to the new home –
but the more ferocious Swiss masters are so dependent,
they require to be carried helplessly in the jaws of their
slaves.[7]

No wonder, then, that the translator of Hans Heinz Ewers's
The Ant People warned his readers of the 1920s that ants were
not to be trusted as Solomon suggested:

Many of our preconceived ideas about ants are exploded
by Dr. Ewers. We find that the ants are not at all industrious as we have been led to believe. We learn that among
the Ants are many species that never work, others that live
by theft, and still others who live like the robber barons of
the Middle Ages. In a word, we may now learn all that the
layman needs to know about Ants, and how they live,
love, work, or loaf, just like some other Peoples.[8]

GIANT ANTS AND OTHER LATER TWENTIETH-CENTURY HORRORS

As the twentieth century progressed so the nature of the enemy
within metamorphosed from a eugenic, degenerative threat.
During the Cold War there were red ants under the bed. The US
B-movie *Them!* (1954), like so many Martian films of its era, constructs the invading enemy as thinly disguised communists.
Corpses evidencing unusual modes of death and traumatized
victims (screaming 'Them! Them!') gradually give the game
away: giant ants are terrorizing the New Mexico desert. They
can send messages among themselves, and kill their victims by
holding them with their mandibles, while administering
enough formic acid to kill 'twenty men'. Killing the super-sized
workers is understandably tricky, and completely futile too, so

long as the queen is hidden underground replenishing her army. Unlike the ants, whose modes of communication are perfect, the film's humans learn rather slowly the military codes and methods necessary to defeat them. The humans' insectan goggles and gas masks are an ironic and imperfect echo of their enemies' nature. Cold War news panics echo round the airwaves and martial law is in place as the intrepid heroes enter the final underground nest in Los Angeles. Meanwhile, it has been established that the mutant ants owe their existence to radiation from an atomic bomb test in the desert, raising the possibility that the fight may only just be beginning. The effects of the Cold War may be poised to destroy America unexpectedly from within, a theme that was reworked in subtler form in *Phase IV* (1973).

opposite: Movie poster for the film *Them!* (1954), a classic giant bug epic.

Drawing their victim into the sand, the deadly ants of *Phase IV* (1973) strike.

One episode of animated comedy, *The Simpsons*, pays humorous homage to insectan 'reds-under-the-bed' films like *Them!* while satirizing their notions of ants as the 'enemy within'. The story goes that the programme's everyman anti-hero, Homer Simpson, has been selected to join a space mission as what the media dubs an 'average-naut'. Once in orbit, an incident involving snack food (which Homer was not supposed to bring on board) leads to his destruction of an experimental ant colony set up to discover 'if ants can be trained to sort tiny screws in space'. Although there is a harmless explanation for the presence of ants, once released, they float directly in front of the on-board camera lens, appearing gigantic due to this chance of perspective. The pictures are beamed to Channel Six's blustering presenter Kent Brockman until, presumably, an ant gets caught in the camera's works and the picture cuts out. In a panicked moment, Brockman turns collaborator:

> Ladies and gentlemen, er, we've just lost the picture, but, uh, what we've seen speaks for itself. The Corvair spacecraft has been taken over – 'conquered' if you will – by a master race of giant space ants. It's difficult to tell from this vantage point whether they will consume the captive earth men or merely enslave them. One thing is for certain, there is no stopping them; the ants will soon be here. And I, for one, welcome our new insect overlords. I'd like to remind them that as a trusted TV personality, I can be helpful in rounding up others to toil in their underground sugar caves.

The satiric genius of this moment lies in the transition from B-Movie images of giant ants to the cowardly response of Brockman, so opposed to the heroic all-American images portrayed in the McCarthyite era, and yet so much more probable. Thus Groening, the show's creator, uses ants to satirize the hysteria and rhetoric surrounding the notion of the enemy within.

The 1990s saw a whole new crop of giant insect movies. Often these films are not terribly specific about the precise kind of species involved but key into well-established tropes about insects' group dynamics, the horror lurking behind the kitchen cupboards of civilization. *Starship Troopers* (1997) was a bloody and controversial example of the genre. American troops queued to join their propagandist military machine and gladly flew to other planets to face death at the slashing claws of massed giant arthropods. Was it a naïve (if exceptionally violent) monster movie? Was it a fascist celebration of militarism? Or was it an ironic portrayal of us nationalism, comparing it to the unthinking mass behaviour of the ant horde? Critics could not make up their minds.

Mimic (1998) can be seen as another film dealing in ant-like symbols, though strictly speaking it is about a mutant termite-cockroach hybrid. This film's threat lurks in the New York subway, that ambivalent symbol of the very heart of the city. The director, Guillermo Del Toro, commented on the alienation that inspired this re-working of the old enemy within theme:

> In every neighbourhood, there are one or two guys in shabby overcoats . . . what if they were not human? What I found intriguing was the idea of us being unaware of an alternate form of life that is breeding and feeding under our noses. We don't realise it because we pay little attention to people on the street at 2 am in the morning [sic]. And when that figure opens up like a fan and becomes like an insect . . . Insects are the dark angels of the Lord

Homer's carelessness with ruffled potato snacks leads to a freak accident involving apparently giant ants in *The Simpsons* (1994).

and one day they will just whack the shit out of us.[9]

Beyond this sense of the threat posed from within by the home-less, shiftless sub-class, *Mimic* yields a feminist reading of the 'enemy within'. The reproducing queen is the most frightening aspect of this film. To underline the point by irony, the scientist who is responsible for the experiment that went wrong is herself trying for a baby throughout the story. The female's desire to reproduce is the subtextual horror of this movie (much like *Species* of 1995), whereas in *Them!* the queen, though the root of the problem, takes up less screen space than the bellicose giant workers.

Even E. O. Wilson, donor of tuna and whipped cream to the ants in his kitchen, has occasionally been rattled by the prospect of ants as the enemy within. In the late 1960s, tiny yellow ants began to appear throughout Harvard's research lab-oratories. They were first discovered when a research assistant found her pipette of sugar solution clogged with the insects.

The serious trouble began when an assistant . . . began the routine pipetting of sugar solution for the culture of bacteria. She could not draw the liquid through. Looking more closely, she saw that the narrow pipette channel was plugged with small yellow ants. Other, more subtle signs of the strange invasion had been noted in the build-ing. Here and there yellow ants quickly covered food left out after lunch or afternoon tea. Portions of breeding colonies . . . appeared miraculously beneath glass vessels, in letter files, and between the pages of notebooks. But most alarming, researchers found the ants tracking faint traces of radioactive materials from culture dishes across the floor and walls. An inspection revealed that a giant unified colony was spreading in all directions through spaces and walls of the large building.[10]

Detective work revealed that the invaders had hitchhiked back from Brazil with one of Wilson's students, infecting the packing cases that contained his intended specimens. By the time the cases were unloaded and the stowaways discovered, the yellow ants had formed a supercolony in the walls of the building and were 'metastasizing'. Wilson's use of a word more commonly associated with a malignant tumour is revealing. Cancer is, after all, the most frightening enemy within. Wilson's silently spreading supercolony was a cancerous growth subverting every aspect of life in the Harvard laboratories, from the recording of information to the execution of experiments, and to humans' social interactions over food. With only a small amount of circumspection, Wilson refers to the incident as 'the revenge of the ants'.

Garden ants (*Lasius niger*) invade the kitchen.

The ants responsible for this episode are known as Pharaoh's ant, and though they originate in the East Indies, they have been known to infest buildings around the world. The secret of their horror lies in the fact that individually they are almost too small to be seen. They have been known to colonize hospitals, crawling across immobilized patients, consuming their damaged flesh and spreading disease.

'When we came to settle here we did not know about the ants.' So begins Italo Calvino's story about a similar experience, 'The Argentine Ant' (1952).[11] A young couple move on the recommendation of the man's uncle and discover that their new residence is infested by ants. They form a seething black scum on top of every container of milk; they stream down the walls and crawl across the couple's sleeping baby, awaking the narrator to its terrified screams. Calvino evokes the powerless horror of seeing everything overrun by such a ridiculously tiny enemy.

Workers of the invading Argentine ant *Iridomyrmex humilis* tend clusters of larvae and eggs in Hawaii.

The word 'ants' for us then could never have even suggested the horror of our present situation. If [Uncle Augusto] had mentioned ants . . . we would have imagined ourselves up against a concrete enemy that could be numbered, weighed, crushed . . . Here we were face to face with an enemy like fog or sand, against which force was useless.[12]

Odder than the ants themselves is the village's mysterious community. Everyone tolerates the ants through forced humour, indifference or silent, tortured pride, pretending that they are unaffected. The couple's neighbour Captain Brauni is obsessed with his ant-killing inventions, each more ineffectual than the last. The 'ant man', representative of the Argentine Ant Control Corporation, comes round every few months to put down poisoned molasses, though all the villagers are in agreement that it does no good – or is even a strengthening tonic for the ants. This man, who is strangely ant-like himself, is discovered to have a dirty, food-strewn shack that appears suspiciously more like a breeding ground for the ants than a control centre.

Like all Calvino's stories, the meanings of this tale are elusive. There is no denouement, no final enactment of horror or resolution of the grotesque situation. Rather, perhaps, Calvino is describing the intangible horrors of domestic life: the loathsome details of existence that are too subliminal for us to notice and address, and which threaten to destroy us from within.

ILLEGAL IMMIGRANT ANTS

Later still in the twentieth century, ants from Latin America 'invaded' the southern states of the US. The two varieties of ant chiefly in question are Calvino's Argentine ants (*Iridomyrmex humilis*) and the fire ant (*Solenopsis invicta*). Reports of these ants' infractions bear more than a passing resemblance to the construction of human immigration problems in the area.

Around the year 1997, Californians began to notice 'ruthless Argentine interlopers' establishing a giant supercolony in their very back yards. The *New York Times* reported the underhand secret of the ants' success: instead of 'fight[ing] with one another the way they do in their homeland' they were co-operating, 'using a united family front to win territory from native ants'. The science writer of the *San Francisco Chronicle* reported that the danger posed by the invading ants even extended to native vertebrates.

In a wonderfully ironic twist, the *New York Times* (1 August 2000) included information on the Argentine ant sourced from an ambivalent expert:

> The Argentine ants get to food faster, overwhelm rivals with sheer numbers of workers and defend their territory with chemical weapons they spray on opponents. 'The Argentine ants win in a few days,' Andrew Suarez, a graduate student, said with grim determination. (Suarez's family came from Argentina.)

Suarez's solution to the invasion is simple, but should the reader trust him? Rip up your lawns, he says; 'You wouldn't have [the ants] if there were native plants and cactus, and San Diego looked like it should.' In other words, says the Argentine, give up your claim to Southern California. Here, then, albeit light-heartedly, Wilson's invading ants are suggested to have teamed up with the most cunning choice of infiltrator: the Argentine ant expert.

Myrmecologist Deborah Gordon takes a more measured view of the invading ants. In one of her research papers, she concludes that the Argentines are no more innately aggressive than the ants they are displacing, in that they do not initiate confrontations with native ants any more frequently than native ants initiate them with the Argentines. Whenever such confrontations are initiated, however, the Argentine is more likely to walk away the victor. Yet even the fact that her research has implicitly been framed in terms of *disproving* the inherent aggression of Argentine ants demonstrates that she has to work within a cultural context that constructs the ants in particular, human terms.

Fire ants, which deliver an extremely unpleasant sting to humans, are an even greater source of anxiety to Americans in the southern states, and correspondingly take up more space in the collective imagination. Their rise to prominence in the Californian media coincided with that of unwanted human immigrants, and similar language was used to describe both

Stings inflicted on a human ankle by a fire ant. The ant grasps the flesh with its jaws, then injects a toxic venom.

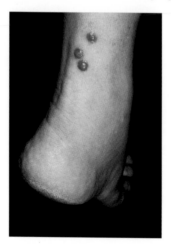

Irresistibly conceived as invaders, these fire ants are portrayed by the *Los Angeles Times* conquering a map of the area.

sets of problems. '[T]he red imported fire ant [is] just that – imported', began one report, bluntly.[13] In 1999, an *LA Times* article estimated that 'in large parts of the San Francisco Bay, aliens account for nine out of ten species'.[14] Likewise, English-speaking Californians were getting their heads around the fact that theirs was becoming a minority language in the state. In 2000, Mexico's President Fox proposed to open further the borders between his country and the US. Outraged correspondents wrote to the *LA Times* protesting 'Americans . . . need breathing room from the army of Mexican nationals streaming across our weakly defended southern border each and every day.'[15]

Both sets of 'invaders' are commonly presented as a drain upon the economy. 'Exotic species are a parasite on the US economy, sapping an estimated $138 billion annually', judged one authority in 1999.[16] A few months later, Orange County, CA, devoted six million dollars to the next eighteen months' fire ant eradication programme. Meanwhile, similar concerns were

The fire ant eradication programme involved dosing ant mounds with pesticide.

being expressed about the cost of human immigration to the taxpayer. In 1994, 60 per cent of Californians had voted in the controversial Proposition 187, which denied public services such as health care to illegal immigrants. This measure died in the courts in 1999, at which point a new initiative was proposed – at exactly the same time as the flurry of invading Central American ant stories. One backer of the new bill explained 'we don't like our country to be invaded and for others to abuse our hard-earned money.'[17] Another wrote: 'The United States cannot be a sponge for Mexico's poor.'[18]

Concerned citizens were mustered on both fronts of invasion, and later reined back when their efforts were deemed to be obstructive or embarrassing. Orange County residents were urged in 1999 to bait and capture any suspect ants, and to send them off for identification or call the County's special hotline, 1-888-4FIREANT. Official advice on how to destroy the nests was later retracted as actually contributing to their spread. Meanwhile, that same year, immigration and state fraud agents were positioned at airports in California and at the

Mexican border to question, identify and net travellers who had received state medical aid contrary to that permitted by their status of residency. In Chandler, Arizona, city leaders were embarrassed at their planned round-up of illegals which ended up netting many citizens who 'looked Mexican'. The outcry following this event damaged the anti-immigrationists' cause.

Another 1990s TV satire, *King of the Hill*, deals with these North American images of concealed formic enmity. In the episode 'King of the Ant Hill', Hank Hill's dream of the perfect lawn is wrecked by an invasion of fire ants, secretly introduced by his jealous neighbour. The neighbour, Dale, is the enemy within; in his basement he hides a scale model of the Hills' house, surrounded by miniature ant hills. The queen ant, meanwhile, soon has Hank's son, Bobby, under her hypnotic control. Dale recants his evil ways at the moment when Bobby is about to be stung to death by the ants, and he heroically interposes his own body as a sacrifice to the vicious stinging swarm.

Whether knowingly or not, the episode draws on a powerful cultural image of south-western American status and paranoia: the lawn itself, that object of Argentine myrmecologist Suarez's scorn. Lawns are a small piece of New England, or England itself, that every Californian, Texan and Arizonan wants in his front yard. This piece of horticultural snobbery persists despite its inappropriacy in a desert climate. Indeed, that is the whole point of the southern states lawn. It demonstrates social status in the form of money to throw at a folly of cultivation. Thus the settlers of the south-western US symbolize their permanence, their parity with the traditionally snobbish north-eastern seaboard, by employing a signifier of 'old' culture. Meanwhile the 'invading' central Americans – the fire ants – must be signified as dangerous 'others'. This is tricky since large parts of the south-western US belonged to Mexico until Texas broke away in 1836 and

The computer game *SimAnt* (1991) enables players to see lawn invasions from the other perspective, by playing as an ant.

In this screen shot from *SimAnt*, the user reviews attempts to grow the colony and overrun the humans' lawn.

further parts were seized by the US in the Mexican War (1846–8; in a double irony, Hank wants his lawn for a Cinco de Mayo party). Historically, the true invaders are the Hills and their neighbours.

The US is not unique in its myrmecological xenophobia. In 2002, a similar story burst upon the Europeans. 'Ant super-colony dominates Europe', proclaimed the BBC.[19] These ants, introduced to Europe about eighty years ago, had established a supercolony across '6000 kilometres from northern Italy through the south of France to the Atlantic coast of Spain, with billions of related ants occupying millions of nests'. What is most remarkable about these ants, like their American cousins, is their degree of cooperation between nests, when they would normally be expected to fight. Thus, wrote the BBC journalist, 'evolution . . . reinforced [their] superiority because [they] had time and resources to fight off their enemies'. Professor Keller of the University of Lausanne, Switzerland, commented: 'This leads to the greatest cooperative unit ever discovered.'

What makes this story so interesting is its political context, suggesting that it may be read as a cautionary tale about that human supercolony, the European Union. It mirrors contemporary issues to do with the growth and consolidation of the EU, at a time when elements of tension, nationalism and doubt grew within it. In 2002, for example, member states' responses to war in Afghanistan continued to be disunited; most were somewhat sceptical about the cause, while Britain threw its weight behind US action. (A similar situation was to ensue in 2003 over the war in Iraq.) In Italy, there was a political murder over the intended imposition of labour laws more in line with Europe. To the chagrin of the French, their presidential run-off took place between Jacques Chirac and extreme right-wing candidate Jean-Marie Le Pen, who stood on a platform of policies including the withdrawal of France from the European Union. Just days earlier, Britons had rued the election of racist, nationalist councillors to some areas of local government, who appealed to voters fearing a dilution of 'English' identity. The UK, of course, has a long history of resisting the European government and its 'Eurocrats', who according to popular wisdom like nothing better than to legislate against elements of British tradition such as T-bone steaks and beer by the pint. In 2002 the British media continued to fret over illegal immigrants (re-named 'bogus asylum seekers' by the tabloid press), now entering direct from France through that feared connection with Europe, the Channel Tunnel.

Amidst this widespread anxiety about European homogeneity, the 'discovery' of a European supercolony speaks to broader cultural issues. The ants become interesting because of the analogies they suggest; they are described – constructed – in terms that reinforce those analogies. Even the introduction of these ants to Europe around the end of the First World War coincides with the period in which the tensions of nation states and the threat of European domination/unification emerged in their modern form. Myrmecologists agree that the same fate may befall the ants' supercolony as commentators predict for the European Union; its cooperation is doomed. 'Sooner or later', one is reported as saying 'rivalries will emerge as genetically distinct groups of ants turn against each other.' A sound clip of Professor Jurgen Heinze warns BBC web site users: 'The supercolony may start to break up.'

It gets better. Spain contains particularly strong regional identities. Indeed, for many of its Basques and other citizens, 'regional' is a misnomer: the term should be 'national'. How perfect then, that within a European Union whose member states struggle to hold together their own nationalist elements, there should be a 'rival Catalan supercolony'. These nationalist ants, based around the Barcelona area, have managed to advance their counter-unification forces as far as half-way along the southern Spanish coastline. It would, of course, be ridiculous to suggest that these ants have evolved or behaved in a way that is dependent upon the contingencies of human history. What is undeniable, however, is that their behaviour has been noticed, reported and described in a particular context of human concerns: concerns that have constructed the nature of these ants for us.

SLY CAPITALIST ANTS

In the global economy, the definition of the enemy within expands greatly. Even an overseas entity can pose a threat within the community of world trade. In 1991, the then French Prime Minister Edith Cresson famously dealt with an economically threatening situation by describing the Japanese as 'like ants'. Her precise words have mutated in various retellings. One particularly harsh recollection gives her words thus: 'The Japanese are like ants, they stay up all night working hard, figuring out how to screw you in the morning.'[20] At first sight, these words have virtually nothing to do with ants; apart from an inexhaustible busyness, it is more a sexual violence that is attributed here to the Japanese. In fact, this statement appears to be a conflation of two comments made one month apart. In the first, Cresson called the Japanese 'a nation of ants'. One month later she reportedly commented that the Japanese were 'little yellow men' who 'stay up all night thinking about ways to screw the Americans and the Europeans.'[21] The combination of these comments in the collective memory was entirely to be expected. Twentieth-century images of ants as threat have long been projected onto any other group likewise perceived as numerous, indistinguishable and dangerous, and have in turn reinforced that construction of the ants themselves.

An Asian magazine tried to put a more positive spin on Cresson's remarks, highlighting ants' natural theological virtues of honour and industry. The comparison was, claimed the author, quite probably intended as a compliment.[22] The improbability of this analysis is underlined by Alan Farrell in his article on representations of the Vietnamese in French colonial literature.[23] He describes the typical orientalist formic image as one of 'long columns of tiny, faceless, straining figures who dragged siege guns, rice bags, artillery rounds through the jungle in filiform legions'. The threatening incomprehensibility of the Vietnamese to the French is expressed most clearly by the novelist Jean Lartéguy, again quoted by Farrell:

> All these ants seemed featureless . . . on their faces could be read no expression at all, not even one of those elemental feelings that break through the passivity of Asiatic features: fear, joy, hate, anger. Nothing. One single will pressed them all on toward a common and mysterious goal . . . This frenzied activity by sexless insects seemed directed from a distance, as if somewhere in this colony, some huge queen was to be found, a sort of monstrous central brain which served as the collective consciousness of these ants.[24]

Cresson's alleged explanation of her original statement plays on similar negative qualities of the ants, as recently perceived in the West.

I said [the Japanese] worked like ants. Ants work a lot, it's true . . . We can't live in minuscule apartments like that, spend two hours commuting to work. And work, work, work, and have children who will work like beasts. We want to keep our social guarantees, live like human beings, as we have always lived.[25]

One can make sense of her statements according to the trope of the enemy within. Quite apart from describing the perceived Japanese threat to the French economy, there is a deeper anxiety hidden within Cresson's words. To compete effectively with the Japanese, she infers, Europeans would have to change their very society, capitulating to the foreign mores of the ants, abandoning all emotion and individuality. It would be just as though the Ant-Japanese had invaded and imposed their rules and customs. This is the essence of the fear of the enemy within.

6 Ants as Machines

Aristotle was not quite sure what to make of ants. He had differentiated three kinds of soul – vegetable, animal and rational – of which the final variety was possessed only by man. This would clearly count against ants performing their actions by means of reason. However, in his *History of Animals*, he claimed that 'just as in man we find knowledge, wisdom and sagacity, so in certain animals there exists some other natural capacity akin to these'.[1] Thus analogy seemed to be the final word in the comparison between humans and animals. Medieval theologians and scholastics elaborated on this analysis. They emphasized the wonder of God's creation, and the fact that He could fashion something like man's greatest attribute – rationality – by entirely different means. By the time of the Enlightenment, the nature of the analogy had changed. Now, a marked similarity was perceived between the behaviour of insects and automatism; ants and bees were the most fascinating examples of this behaviour, for their machine-like acts enabled them to sustain and operate complex societies. Later still, as technology became more threatening, ants underwent a corresponding transformation in their representation. The first work about robots, *R.U.R.*, modelled its protagonists on human versions of ant workers, while *Metropolis* was among other films and novels showing human life as an underground, antish hell. Recently it has become more fashionable for scientists to base artificial intelligence on organic models; the ant-machine has once again been transformed in its nature, this time into an inspirational and trustworthy model for technology – and even the human mind itself.

If animals, as Descartes claimed, were effectively automata, then ants were one of the more intriguing models of nature's machines. Curiously, atheist mechanists and theists produced virtually indistinguishable accounts of ant behaviour. Whether or not they were designed by God, these little creatures provided examples of incredibly precise actions. Whether or not God was pulling the strings of these tiny marionettes, no human artificer could replicate the results.

The metaphysical writings of Julien Offray de La Mettrie were a two-fold provocation intended to puncture the ego of humans, particularly arrogant philosophers and religionists. On the one hand, as he argued in *Machine Man* (1747), all human actions and dispositions could be reduced to mechanical phenomena; on the other, he went on to deny man's supposed superiority to the animals in *Animals More than Machines* (1750). Thus La Mettrie made man a machine; animals, men; and, although only by extension, what Descartes had argued: animals, machines. In short, humans were scarcely superior to the ant: '[Nature's] power shines out as clearly in the creation of the meanest insect as in that of the most splendid human.' In a sly further argument he pretended to accept the immortality of the soul, with which he equated the rationality of man, – provided that the reader would also allow one for each and every insect:

To insist that an immortal machine is a paradox or a *being of reason* is as absurd a deduction as would be that of caterpillars if, on seeing the remains of their fellow caterpillars, they lamented the bitterly the fate of their species which was apparently dying out. The souls of these insects (for each animal possesses its own) are too limited to understand nature's metamorphoses . . . We are the same.[2]

Gilles Bazin, a French writer working in the same decade, had a more generous perspective on the relationship between insect, human and machine. His lengthy treatise on bees (1744), written as a dialogue between a young landed lady, Clarissa, and her knowledgeable friend, Eugenio, repeatedly emphasized the machine-like qualities of these close relatives of the ants, while gently but firmly delineating their behaviour from the majority of human action for this very reason. Eugenio reassures Clarissa that the bees will not harm her by emphasizing that they are not liable to wilful aggression like humans: 'These are not men, but animals, instructed by nature, and faithful to their instructions; animals, that do not suffer themselves to be hurried away by the movements of an irregular passion.'[3] The theme of this, Clarissa's early correction, is returned to several times by the author. Each time he makes the point more forcefully that bees are mechanical creatures, operating according to the cogs of instinct placed within them by God. Clarissa, astonished to learn that the newly pupated bee is instantly mature and 'knows all it has to do for the rest of its life', remarks 'How happy should we be, if he, who formed our children, had given them to us perfectly instructed!' Once more, Eugenio points out the difference between humans and insects in this respect:

René Antoine Ferchault de Réaumur (1683–1757) studying ants. Réaumur's understanding of insect behaviour informed Bazin's work.

Take care, Clarissa, not to complain unjustly: he would have given you nothing but machines, instead of docile children, as yours are: he would have deprived you of the most sensible and the most soothing of all pleasures, that a mother can have, that of conducting them yourself to virtues by your counsels and your examples.[4]

By the end of the book, Clarissa – whose learning process echoes that intended for the reader – has made two sustained arguments of her own that classify bees as machines, thus differentiating them from humans. In the following speech, Clarissa responds to the complex geometry and precise workmanship of the bees' hexagonal cells:

I have been ever since [our last conversation] figuring to my fancy, a Bee, handling its materials in the same manner as an artificer would do; cutting lozenges under certain determined angles; and discovering the utmost thriftiness with regard to the disposal of the wax. As I imagined to myself this insect busied in its work; pursuing its ends with certainty, and this by the best means, I was perfectly tempted to allow them judgment or reason; and even a series of argumentation, such as are necessary for man . . . In the extasy to which this raised me, I was asham'd to see myself obliged to yield, in the article of understanding, to insects.

However, an analogy from music occurs to Clarissa, preventing her from accepting her initial thoughts on the matter:

It frequently happens to me, whilst I am sitting by my Harpsichord, to play on it, without once reflecting on

what I am doing . . . My fingers once set agoing, shall perform of themselves a work almost equal to a cell; and
execute the whole quite mechanically. I then will boast
my having formed automaton-fingers, fingers which play
a harpsichord-air, without my . . . reasoning faculty having any thing to do with them. Now, why should we
imagine the Almighty has not the same power; I mean
that of creating animals capable of executing, without the
faculty of reason, such works as are most complicated,
and require the greatest industry.[5]

Eugenio praises her analogy, and explains that bees, moreover, can correct their cells – a feat so amazing it were as though
a harpsichordist could substitute new harmonies around false
notes. Thus their automatisms are actually superior to humans'.

No human reason, how enlightened and sagacious soev-
er, comes into the world with such talents [as the bee].
Our insects are a proof, that, if the author of their Being
has refused them an understanding like to that of man;
he has compensated for it, by sending them into the
world ready instructed; and much better instructed than
if he had left to them (as is done to human creatures) the
care of instructing themselves.[6]

Thus by the end of the book, Clarissa and the reader have
learned that insects are given 'instructions' by God rather than
learning by human counsel and reasoning. They have come to
appreciate that insects are so impressive they give humans
pause for thought before taking pride in their own abilities.
Whether atheist or theist, many Enlightenment writers agreed
that the engine of the animal machine was what we would

now call instinct. Whether interpreted as naturalistic or God-given, this formed a counterpoint to human hubris.

By the twentieth century, the cosy assumptions of the natural theologians' 'happy world' (Chapter 3) had disappeared. There was no particular reason to assume that humans possessed anything more than mechanical instinct. Nor, as Freud argued, was there any particular reason to assume that those instincts were trustworthy. No wonder, then, that in this period we see works of literature dealing fearfully with the notion that human society might be as mechanistic as the ants'.

E. M. Forster's early story 'The Machine Stops' (1909) is a work of science fiction, and it suggests that human instinct is in some way like, or is becoming like, the ants'. The thing that underlines humans' similarity to insects in this tale is their adjustment to a mechanically directed way of life. Forster's sense of alienation from modern city life has been well documented; in this story he represents his urban dystopia as something in between a beehive (each individual inhabits a separate hexagonal cell) and an ants' nest (the commune is underground). Each person exists entirely within his cell; all physical needs are provided for by the machine. Entertainment and communication between individuals also come via the machine. (Indeed, it's very tempting to read the tale ahistorically as an anticipation of the Internet.)

The story's central character resists the de-individualization that accompanies his form of life. He communicates with his mother, asking for a meeting between them, and she responds in perplexity that by using the machine they *are* meeting. The mother's dogmatic adherence to the norms of the machine suggests the symbolic control of the queen ant. The hero's final destruction comes from two quarters at once. His repeated efforts to go outside the city-nest make him an object of suspicion, and put him at risk; the reader has the sense that if things were to go on like this, he would bring his own fate upon himself. But what finally finishes the hero, and the rest of his ant-world with him, is the failure of the machine itself. The members of Forster's society, mechanically adjusted to their mechanical world, cannot survive the breakdown of their system, and all perish together.

The Czech writer Karel Čapek (1890–1938), like his contemporary Franz Kafka, was inspired to write about insects as a reflection on the human condition. He dealt twice with ants, once in his anthropomorphic *The Insect Play* (1921) and once in *R.U.R.* (1921). In *The Insect Play* (co-written with his brother Josef), human frailties are satirized by comparing them to the foibles of insects; the dung beetle represents the dull material ambition of the petit bourgeoisie, and the butterflies the frivolousness of flirtatious young people. The tramp who has been watching all these insects disport themselves comments that at least humans distinguish themselves by their noble ability to work together. No sooner has he said this than the final act gets underway; in it, ants embody the play's bloodiest aspects of humanity, for they fight a vicious and pointless battle to the death, each individual mindlessly following the lunatic instructions of his [sic] leader. As a blind ant counts them off to war, the tramp comments, 'They all move in time as he counts, one, two, three, four. Like machines – Bah, it makes my head swim.' The ants' horror lies in the mechanical nature of their obedience, and in the resemblance of this to human behaviour, especially during the decade prior to the play's first performance.

Karel Čapek's *R.U.R.*, first performed in 1921, also takes a political angle on the question of human mechanization and its similarity to formicarian life. The play is based on a verbal conceit conflating humans and ants; the word 'robot', introduced to the world by this work, is Czech for 'drudge', or 'worker', and thus refers to both species. In Čapek's tale, the mechanized workers have been created by the evil technician Rossum as the perfect labourers, with no component that does not contribute directly to the progress of work, such as playing the violin or going for walks. Like 'The Machine Stops', the play also contains a queen-like character: Helena, the daughter of the robot-making company's president. Helena is partly responsible for stirring up the robots' revolt with her misguided message of liberation. Condemned to mechanical servitude, yet thirsty for life, the robots eventually rise up and overthrow their maker's race. The mistake made by Rossum and his colleagues is that they have denied the true force of life within themselves in the pursuit of

opposite: The Čapek Brothers' *Insect Play* (1921) depicted ants as mindless, robotic soldiers, as shown here in this recent costume design by Lucas Haley.

Fritz Lang's *Metropolis* (1927) had underground workers reminiscent of ants.

mechanized efficiency. Thus they have inadvertently created robots in their own spirit-less image; because they deny the urge for life in themselves, they do not realize that it will inevitably emerge in these new beings, and what its results will be.

Metropolis, filmed by Fritz Lang in 1925–6, deals with similar themes. Once again, this features a subterranean army of workers; this time they are human, albeit degraded. Another strong female character, Maria, guides the underground tribe through her hypnotic, yet gentle, leadership. Another evil scientist attempts to create an automaton, but this time the idea is to make a fake Maria, who will be able to steer the populace according to the wishes of its maker, and against the interests of the overworked masses. The scientist's assumption – which the film does not contradict – is that the workers can be manipulated like ants, if only he can create an automatized queen. Unlike Forster's story, this film seems not to condemn, but rather to pity the mechanized workers in their thoughtless, lifeless condition.

In one way or another, these works all speak to early twentieth-century fears about the relationship between humans and ants, specifically as this was constructed from contemporary metaphors of machinery and mechanism. Čapek, at times, predicts the triumph of the life force, while Lang and Forster are less sanguine about the fate of humans in their modern, mechanized, ant-like life.

ANTS AND THE BEAUTY OF SYSTEMS

Some time after the Second World War, a new way of thinking began to emerge. Combining philosophy, mathematics, psychology, computing and information science with entomology, it put forward holism as a good and useful way of looking at the world. There had been a philosophical vogue for holist thinking from

152

the 1910s to the late 1930s, but now this was resurrected in the context of emerging computer technology. One of the key papers from that earlier period, 'The Ant-Colony as an Organism' was also 'rediscovered' and interpreted, somewhat out of context, as a precursor for the new thinking.[7] The behaviour of the ant colony and other organic processes were lauded as the model for proper knowledge. Culturally it was an odd phenomenon; on the one hand the impetus for the development of information theory had been the military and cryptographic paranoia of the Cold War, yet on the other hand it responded to the anti-reductionist outlook of the post-war counter-culture. M. C. Escher's strange, tessellating designs reflect this new-found beauty in the looping, chemically encrypted systems of ant organization. Following his contact with the mathematician and holist philosopher Roger Penrose, Escher designed 'Möbius Strip II (Red Ants)', explicitly symbolizing the new philosophy with a formic figure. Escher had previously been sufficiently interested by ants and other insects in the 1940s to draw detailed enlargements of them. The non-logical yet perfect constructions of social insects (the beehive, the ant hill), suggested Escher's self-taught, intuitive approach to problems of symmetry.

Douglas Hofstadter's *Gödel, Escher, Bach* (1979) was perhaps the high watermark of the first phase of this renaissance of holist science and creativity, before the information revolution overtook the lives of the general public. His chapter 'Prelude . . . Ant Fugue' uses ants' organization as the theme for a baroque discussion about the ways to understand the different levels in a system. It is cleverly modelled on the conceit that, when listening to a fugue, one can either follow each line individually or enjoy the overall sound, but not both at once. In the same way, watching an individual ant will never reveal anything about the organization of its nest as a whole. Dr Anteater explains how he

Escher's looping
designs, such as
this 1963 wood-
cut, *Möbius Strip II
(Red Ant),*
inspired counter-
cultural innova-
tion in artificial
intelligence.

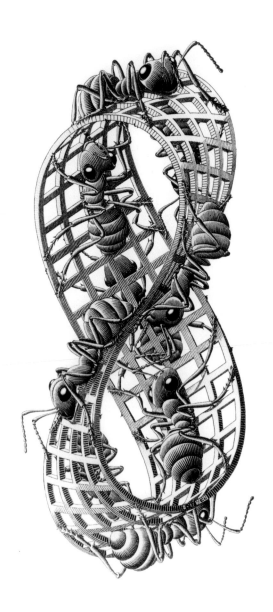

observes a whole colony 'Aunt Hillary', much to the mystifica-
tion of his friends. Although the individual ants are brainless,
together their actions have a significance, which, viewed from
above, can be read. Dr Anteater even claims to be Aunt Hillary's
interlocutor; by intervening in her group actions, he conveys
meaningful information to the nest, to which it responds by
changing those behaviours.

Together Dr Anteater and his friends inspect visual riddles –
small letters grouped to make larger letters – which like the ant
colony yield different meanings according to the level on which
they are viewed. Hofstadter's explanation, added for the republi-
cation of the chapter in *The Mind's I* (1981) elaborates on these
themes. We are used to making sense of things by looking at
them from the ground up, he argues, but looking down on the

M. C. Escher's
1943 lithograph,
Ant, an early
example of the
insectan theme
that was to inspire
his explorations
of symmetry and
pattern, and
through these,
philosophy.

system as a whole is also a valid way of understanding, as Dr Anteater demonstrates. There is a downward causation from the colony that makes ants fight back when attacked, or nurse more offspring in times of plenty, or consume some of them in times of want. Granted, there is some kind of pheromonal trigger that makes each ant start or stop a particular task, but there is also a global 'reason' why that trigger, and hence the altered action, is produced. This is a version of teleology that has been rescued from theism; strictly, one ought to maintain scepticism about the nature or creator of the system that appears to make sense from a perspective of 'designed' function. Evolution provides the new, cautious explanation for the appearance of design. Because a function has survived thus far, there must be a good evolutionary reason why it has done so. This in turn predicts probable future success, provided the world does not change too drastically.

Nature has selected for the 'higher-level momentum' of the ants' nest, the thing that keeps it organized in a way that makes sense to the myrmecologist but not to the individual ant. In other words, nature selects for the colony's representational or informational system, the 'active, self-updating collection of structures organized to "mirror" the world as it evolves'.[8] Hofstadter posits the top-down tasks of the ants' nest as being like the function of a computer's purposeful algorithm. Thus, for Hofstadter, the ant hill became an idealized informational system, far in advance of 1980s computer technology: one which was self-reading and self-updating, like human consciousness itself. The ant hill was an optimistic celebration of what philosophers hoped (justifiably, as it transpired) the new technology might achieve.

Hofstadter's musings have gone on to inspire many since the early days of the information revolution. His holist, non-mechanical vision of technology, radically different from that of early twentieth century commentators, has provoked thought that all kinds of things might evolve as organic networks, just like the ants. In the last couple of years, books have been published suggesting that the World Wide Web, Artificial Intelligence and even human cities may all be self-updating systems like the formic colony. This myrmecological/information theory view of evolution persists despite the attempts of reductionists to insist that evolution can only take place when there is a mechanism for passing on successful code to a new generation – in other words, genes. Ants have also come to serve as very specific models for solutions in informational problems, to which topic the remainder of this chapter is devoted.

It was apparently an Italian group of researchers who first thought of ants as a way of solving computational problems.[9]

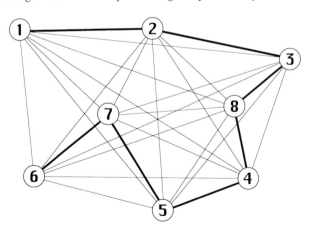

The travelling salesman problem: each node (standing for a city) must be visited once and only once, with the shortest overall path being taken. In this example, possible routes are shown by grey lines, while the solution route is shown in black.

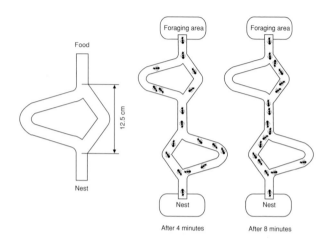

In this 1980s experimental set-up, ants solve a simplified version of the travelling salesman problem for real. After eight minutes, most have settled on the most direct route.

Food

12.5 cm

Nest

Foraging area

Nest

After 4 minutes

Foraging area

Nest

After 8 minutes

The challenge, the so-called 'travelling salesman problem', was to find the quickest route between ten cities, with the proviso that each place should only be visited once. The team posited that the problem could be given a good (if not perfect) solution if they imagined that it was solved by virtual ants, or 'vants', as they were quickly dubbed. The idea was that each vant would wander out at random; the quicker it completed a path the stronger would be the pheromone trail it left behind. The pheromone meant 'walk here' to other vants, so subsequent ones would therefore be more likely to follow that section of the route. The process was repeated 5000 times, after which an optimal route had emerged, followed by all vants.

The Italians' ant algorithms have subsequently been instantiated in the form of hardware design. A laboratory at the Massachusetts Institute of Technology has been working on a community of microrobots.[10] Inspired by ants, they aimed to use the interactions of robots measuring one cubic inch to

Robotic ant that can act as part of a team. The extending wires are touch sensors.

fulfil group tasks. The scientists began by getting the ants to play games such as Follow the Leader; eventually they were able to synthesize a coordinated mine-clearance operation using the little mechanical ants.[11]

In 1997 British Telecommunications (BT) hired entomologists to help solve some of the problems of their massive information network.[12] The phone network needed overhauling, the miles of copper wire to be replaced with optical fibre. Rather like painting the Forth Bridge, the task would need restarting and updating even before it was completed. In addition to this, parts of the system were already failing when under pressure, such as the high number of mobile phone calls from a major motorway jam. What was needed was a high speed, flexible, 'intelligent' way to re-route calls through the system, instead of having fixed pathways through a complex network.

Something like the old faith in animal instinct inspired the decision to bring in the entomologists. The head of research explained: 'Biological organisms do complex things with very simple software, while man's unbelievably complex systems can only do very simple things.' The rationale was that by modelling the network on an ant colony, it too could evolve its own appropriate responses, and become self-governing. One software programme sends out thousands of 'ants', test signals, around a damaged network to find out which alternate route from A to B is fastest. Each 'ant' returns almost instantly, and the information on each journey time feeds back into the network, which reconfigures the connection automatically 'in less than a second', where human operators would take several minutes.

Interestingly, the researchers behind such projects eagerly describe their myrmecological models as the means to create a virtual online environment. 'People will be walking around online in the early 21st century', insisted the BT boss. His dream of a self-made, controllable, alternate reality is not too far from the fantasy kingdom of the anthill. In terms of technological inspiration, ants have swung back around from a negative to a desirable role model. Yet a tension remains within the metaphor, for as one writer points out, the more we design self-sustaining, ant-like computational systems, the more we actually renounce our own control over their evolution and, perhaps, our own futures.

At the heart of research like this, however, lies the profound conviction that there is some essential commensurability between ants and information networks, and that this deep-rooted similarity underwrites the success of computer technology. Moreover, it implies that such technology may provide a useful way to gain insight back into myrmecological processes, as the following examples demonstrate.

On the shores of Lake Geneva, a team of ecologists is planning for a Mars landing. More precisely, they are planning for

Ant robots in Laurent Keller's Geneva laboratory cooperate to perform team tasks.

Keller's ant-robots may one day work together on Mars.

an automated landing; cosmonaut machines will explore the red planet and report back for us. The team writes: 'One of the greatest challenges in robotics is to create machines that are able to interact with unpredictable environments in real time.' A single robot, however, can only learn about one spot at a time and is, moreover, prone to damage. Therefore, the team concludes, 'a possible solution may be to use swarms of robots behaving in a self-organized manner, similar to workers in an ant colony'.[13] These they set about creating. The resultant robots were able to access information about the 'energy level' of the colony, and when this fell below a certain level – a level which varied from individual to individual – they would go out and search for radio tagged 'food items'.

The Geneva group has discovered a couple of important factors governing the efficacy of group organization. First, they found that there was an optimal group size in each experimental set-up (generally around three). A more numerous group did not function any more effectively because of the higher number of chance encounters between robots, interfering with the food gathering function. This they compare to observational findings among certain ants and wasps, which are also found to have reduced worker efficiency in larger colonies. Second, they found that efficiency was much improved when robots were given the capacity to recruit one another to clustered food sources – another obvious parallel with the behaviour of live ants.

Both these findings, then, echo our understanding of how insect societies function. They are also somewhat circular, for the experimental set-up relied in the first place on the group's understanding of ants. For the student of culture, however, what is notable is the sheer strength of this assumption about ants' success in group activity. So powerful is this belief that it forms the basis for a human endeavour as esoteric as space exploration, and stands unqueried as the basis of general conclusions about group behaviour and function in nature.

Dartington, Devon, seems another unlikely location for cutting edge research in artificial intelligence. Home to a multi-disciplinary art college, it is based just outside Totnes, an old market town where the decade of the 1960s appears to have settled down in person to live out its days in gentility, and where healing crystals and organic vegetables fill the shops. Yet the new information theory is oddly at home in such a place. It combines an enthusiasm for the latest, smartest technology with a faith in organic models as its basis. There is something pleasingly counter-cultural in the notion that 'mere' insects could be the best designers of computers, the very things that are supposedly the peak of human ingenuity.

Brian Goodwin, resident scholar at Schumacher College, Dartington, was interested to see whether he could model virtual ants that behaved in similar collective patterns to those observed by his myrmecological colleagues at the

Nigel Franks (University of Bath) sucks up ants with his 'pooter' device ready to study their robot-like teamwork.

Universities of Bath and Houston. In doing so, he hoped to understand something more about the factors explaining the evolutionary fitness of ants (in this case, the genus *Leptothorax*).[14]

Together with two colleagues, he obtained some interesting results. One had noticed that ants go through cycles of activity and inactivity, a fact which is assumed to produce an even, reliable distribution of care of the young. How might these phases be coordinated? They posited that each individual ant might have a random pattern of activity and inactivity, but that it could be shifted from a state of inactivity to activity if it came into contact with an active colleague. To answer this question, they created a computer model. They created a grid each of whose cells was filled with one 'ant' changing at random between active and inactive. If an ant in adjacent cell was active, it too would be tipped over into the active state. However, this pattern would mean that every single ant would quickly be put into a permanently active state. Therefore, the probability of any given ant responding to an active neighbour had to be less than one. If too low, then no pattern emerged. However, if it was too high (but less than one) the pattern was chaotic. But if Goodwin and his colleagues got the sensitivity within the right range, then a rhythm of unpredictable phase emerged. This, suggests Goodwin, gives a mechanism by which a robust emergent feature of colonial life gives rise to survival value. His central claim is that 'the study of emergent phenomena . . . shift[s] the emphasis from genes and fitness to emergent order as a primary source of evolutionary novelty.' What we see in the nest is group behaviour, an emergent phenomenon not uniquely dictated by the genes of the participating ants. Their varied sensitivity, however, he assumes to be genetically encoded, a starting condition for the trial that echoes the Geneva team's

A scanning electron micrograph of an ant holding a microchip. The image suggests the combination of technological progressivism and organic Romanticism that informs current ant-based artificial intelligence.

inbuilt 'genetic' variation in individual robot sensitivity to nest depletion of energy.

The interesting point of contact between the two experiments is this: where the Geneva team assumed that technology would be optimized if it could mimic ants, Goodwin's group assumed that the natural analogy between the two would mean that a successful computer model was bound to reveal how ants do the same process for real. Both groups demonstrate a great faith in the problem-solving ability of nature's systems, and their essential similarity with human informational systems. Kevin Kelly, editor of high-technology magazine *Wired*, wrote *Out of Control* in the mid-1990s, tying together these threads of technophilia and what E. O. Wilson terms consilience – the natural affinity of all living organisms. What Kelly described, and what all these studies exemplify, was a strange but still influential combination of technological progressivism and organic Romanticism.

A biological reductionist would make short work of an argument like Goodwin's: if the evolutionary novelty (group behaviour) is to be passed to the next generation, then whatever it is that makes it possible *must* be encoded in the genes. Otherwise the success of the behaviour is of no long-term or evolutionary significance. But the very persistence of this contradiction indicates how potent is this current combination of ant and machine. Despite the protestations of reductionists, this remains an open debate, and the anti-reductionist viewpoint continues to produce useful and innovative technological solutions. Ants are still a confounding source of wonder, as they were for Aristotle.

7 The Ambiguous Ant

The sun rises over a classic US cityscape, casting its skyscrapers into silhouette. Woody Allen's voiceover monologue echoes the anxieties of every stressed-out office worker at the turn of the twenty-first century. He feels worthless, a tiny cog in a vast machine. As the sun rises further, we see that the high-rises are nothing of the sort; they are actually blades of grass made metropolitan by a trick of the light and the close-up photography (or the appearance thereof – *AntZ* is a film that is computer generated throughout). The viewer pans down to the roots of the grass, down to the earth and under. Finally, the camera comes to light on Allen's character himself, the eponymous, anonymous Ant Z-4195. 'The whole system makes me feel insignificant', Z tells his therapist. The shrink replies that Z has made a breakthrough. 'I have?' he asks. 'Yes', comes the ruthless reply, 'you *are* insignificant.' Thereupon, the camera sweeps round into a vast cavern, the setting for Z's neuroses, which on closer inspection turns out to be a humming, heaving ants' nest, filled with a million workers going about their organized labour.

Z-4195 raises a venerable metaphysical question: what worth does a human life have? In the twentieth century, the era of totalitarian government, the question was framed more precisely: how much individuality does a human being really have? In answering this question through a comparison with ants,

Sunrise in the film *AntZ* reveals a formic cityscape.

the film's makers unwittingly tapped into a fierce debate going on in myrmecology at that very moment – a debate that still rumbles on at the time of writing. 'The ambiguous ant' maps current myrmecological uncertainty about ant autonomy onto the wider contemporary western debate about the individual's place in late capitalist society, using *AntZ* as the common focus for both sets of questions. In doing so, the chapter echoes numerous historical accounts of science that emphasize the essential cultural dimension of all theory and practice.

WILSON V. GORDON

Though not the stuff of newspaper headlines, the dispute between Deborah Gordon and E. O. Wilson has been a prominent row within myrmecology, and has divided its participants rather bitterly over the past ten years or so. On the surface of things, it is a debate about the amount of flexibility in ant behaviour, with Wilson and his allies claiming a fairly rigid relationship between an ant's caste and its specified behavioural function within the nest. Gordon, on the other hand, sees ant behaviour as less fixed, less purposeful and more random. Beneath these seemingly technical disagreements, however, lie a host of personal, social and cultural differences, which have silently defined the corners of the fight and contributed to its unpleasantness.

In the blue corner of the myrmecologists' fight stands Edward O. Wilson, grand old man of natural history, born in 1929 in Alabama, America's deep South. His background, as he gladly acknowledges, was socially conservative, and he thanks his education at the Gulf Coast Military Academy for developing in him qualities of loyalty, discipline and self-sacrifice, subsequently practised in the cause of science. Since his PhD

left: Deborah M. Gordon (born 1955), myrmecologist and behavioural ecologist.

right: Edward Osborne Wilson (born 1929), myrmecologist and pioneer of sociobiology.

days he has been based at Harvard University, 'my destiny', home of the US intellectual elite and the enormous ant collection started in the early twentieth century by William Morton Wheeler. Throughout his career, which he has described as that of a 'naturalist', or 'evolutionary' or 'traditional biologist', Wilson has focused on ants, using them as a model to elaborate evolutionary theory. This project culminated in his 1975 comparative zoological treatise *Sociobiology*. Though criticized by many for naturalizing, and hence justifying, such ugly phenomena as racism and sexism, the book went on to inspire the new generation of evolutionary psychologists. In 1990 Wilson and his colleague Bert Hölldobler published a massive monograph on ants, for which they won the Pulitzer prize. Wilson is now Professor Emeritus at Harvard, and active in the cause of biodiversity preservation.

In the red corner stands Deborah M. Gordon. Born in 1955, she researched for a time at Harvard and Oxford, and is now Associate Professor at Stanford University (a position that Wilson turned down in 1958). Gordon's research area is behavioural ecology, and, like Wilson, she focuses on ants in order to answer what she regards as the most important questions in her field. While Wilson thanks his military teachers for his role models and inspiration in life, Gordon is on record as acknowledging her mother as being her 'closest, strongest mentor'.[1] She shares with Wilson at least one simple motive for her career: a desire to be close to nature and study the creatures that had first fascinated her in childhood. Gordon also considered music, history and philosophy as alternative vocations. Either way, as she has commented lightheartedly, she 'didn't want to have to get dressed up every day and wear uncomfortable shoes [but] wanted to spend time talking about ideas rather than money'. Gordon's first book, *Ants at Work*, was published in 1999 to considerable interest and acclaim.

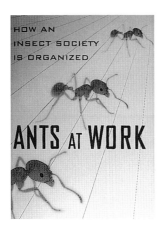

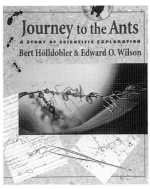

Cover of Deborah Gordon's *Ants at Work* (1999).

Cover of Bert Hölldobler and Edward O. Wilson's *Journey to the Ants* (1994).

Gordon fired an early shot – whether or not intentionally – in 1994. Writing in *Nature*, she opened her review of Wilson's book *Journey to the Ants* (co-written with Bert Hölldobler) with something of a barbed compliment: 'Hölldobler and Wilson have done for ants what Levis did for denim.' Ironically, the pair's publishers put this comment on the back cover of their book, presuming that potential readers would see it as a recommendation, keying into notions of popularization and accessibility. But reading on through Gordon's review, a different set of connotations emerge: uniformity and the ruthlessness associated with global capitalist domination.

Gordon wrote:

> The ants [in *Journey to the Ants*] always know exactly what they are doing. They do not mess around; their duties and their destinies are clear. 'Relentless' and 'fanatical', they are 'self-sacrificing . . . minions programmed to act in concert', 'gangs of factory workers' whose 'loyalty is nearly total' . . . [T]hey are led into servitude by the inexorable hand of natural selection.[2]

On top of this, Gordon hinted at the feminist critique of Wilson's sociobiology, quoting suggestively from his description of the queen ant, a '"demanding beggar", "psychologically reduced" and physically incapable'.

The kernel of Gordon's reservations about the book (in which she also saw much beauty, appeal and worthwhile didacticism) was that its authors were overly inclined to treat ants as fixed – and successfully so – in their behaviour. She commented that other biologists were finding it more revealing to examine 'the function of ant ineptitude'. Gordon has claimed elsewhere that it is often the random component of ant behaviour that allows short-term response to changing circumstances, and in the long term, adaptation. Ants with fixed behaviour, she implies, are sitting targets for natural selection when their environment or ecology changes.

In 1996, writing again in *Nature* (perhaps the best and most prestigious vehicle for taking a debate or piece of research out of one's specialism and into the scientific community at large), Gordon expanded upon her critique.[3] This piece, a review of research on the organization of insect colonies, used Wilson and his colleagues' claims as the straw man against which more recent projects weighed. Gordon centred her review around the question: what makes a worker ant perform one particular task rather than another? From the 1970s until the mid-1980s, she wrote, 'research emphasized the internal factors within an individual that determine its task'. This period, of course, covers the heyday of sociobiology, and Gordon cited a book co-written by Wilson as the exemplar of this school of thought.

Older myrmecologists, Gordon claimed, had wrongly looked at various internal behavioural factors such as polymorphism, the presence in the nest of workers in different shapes and sizes, each of which was suited to, and stuck to, a particular task. Other factors formerly considered to have primary influence upon an ant's career were its age – it might change tasks as it got older – or its genetics. Instead of focusing on such internal factors, Gordon wrote, researchers had now rightly turned to considering external prompts for behaviour. In support of this claim, she cited experiments where intervention in the colony's make-up perturbed worker activity. By removing workers, or otherwise altering the nest conditions, researchers were able to change the tasks performed by workers, thus proving that they were not blindly, internally programmed to do one thing only. On a more theoretical level,

Gordon went on to discuss different possible models for what, precisely, the extrinsic influences on worker behaviour might be. The two principal options were interactions with other workers – a natural feedback loop – and direct environmental influence. She concluded that more experimental work was necessary to decide what the balance was between these factors in nature.

Wilson's allies were quick to respond to these criticisms of their hero. When Gordon's book was reviewed in *Nature* in 1998, the writer used it as an opportunity to attack her and defend Wilson.[4] He claimed that Wilson had never held the opinion that task allocation boiled down merely to polymorphism. Yet Gordon herself admitted in her 1996 paper that 'most researchers have moved beyond the idea of division of labour among innate specialized castes' and that her generalizations simply 'provided a starting point for the study of task allocation'. It is easy to see, however, that the general reader might take such a simplistic reading away from Wilson. For instance, in the Tansley lecture of 1985, Wilson explained that ants have been ecologically successful because 'individual ants can specialize on particular steps, moving from one object (such as a larva to be fed) to another (a second larva to be fed)'.[5] And non-specialist readers who might make this mistaken interpretation were, after all, those whom Gordon addressed in *Ants at Work* – the opus supposedly under review.

Gordon's reviewer also upbraided her for announcing as news that the queen ant is not ruler of the nest. I can confirm since researching this book that this is indeed an unfamiliar fact to a large proportion of the general public, for whom Gordon wrote. The reviewer could not have been unaware of the absurdity of his charge; the powerlessness of the queen has been known since the nineteenth century. His point thus slid into a gibe about writing for an uneducated audience, with a sneering acknowledgement that such explanations were appropriate for the 'naïve reader whose knowledge does not go much beyond the film *AntZ*'. (Gordon, meanwhile, had described *Journey to the Ants* as pitched at the 'educated lay audience'.)

This slippage between criticism and target, rebuttal and critic, suggests that there is more to the debate than the purely objective. Historians of science since Thomas Kuhn have been emphasizing that scientific disagreements can rarely if ever be reduced to logic, and in the following section some of those tacit, cultural differences are brought to the fore. Behind Gordon's attack on the pre-programmed nature of Wilson's ants lies a second, implied critique: that Wilson sneakily respects the ants for their strict regimentation, and recommends it as a model for humans. To put the matter a different way, Wilson is charged with reading his militaristic values into the creatures he studies. Gordon writes: '[U]navoidably, [Hölldobler and Wilson] describe ants in a way consistent with the research programme that they created, a programme devoted to a vision of well-regulated ant societies based on hereditary caste.' Certainly, her analysis of Wilson's choice of language and metaphor is a representative and convincing one. The historian or sociologist of science would agree with Gordon's assessment – and extend it to her own work as well.[6] Gordon's comments, highlighting differences in approach between herself and Wilson, reveal that her work has a different outlook in terms of scientific practice, and in its attitudes towards gender, labour and society.

TACIT ASPECTS OF THE DEBATE: STYLES OF RESEARCH

A close reading of *Journey to the Ants* alongside *Ants at Work* yields two different interpretations of scientific research. The

Patient desert research: zoologists in Tunisia study how ants navigate their zigzag paths using polarized light from the blue sky as a compass.

books' very titles imply something of this; for Wilson, myrmecology is a heroic huntsman's quest, while for Gordon it is a patient act of watching ants' everyday lives. Wilson frequently plays up the gung-ho aspect of collecting; in the following extract he describes part of a youthful expedition to the South Pacific:

> I was afraid, at times, of a crippling accident . . . but most of all of the inexpressible unknown. Would I fail from physical incapacity or lack of will? Would I have to turn back . . .? . . . Why had I come here anyway, except to say I was the first white man to climb the central Sarawaget? . . . I wanted the unique experience of being the first naturalist to walk on the alpine savanna of this part of the Sarawaget crest and collect animals there.[7]

One senses from Wilson's autobiography that he would rather perhaps have been an army man, had not his blindness in one eye precluded him from enlistment. He dwells on his physical

A harvester ant, such as Gordon studies, carrying a thistle seed.

condition with ambivalence; ants are sometimes down-played as organisms suited to a researcher of physical and mental limitations, and other times described as requiring such courage and fortitude in their pursuit as the nineteenth century's explorers possessed. By contrast, Gordon has not played David Livingstone. Instead she has looked at a rather small number of species, and in less exotic conditions. Her most sustained research has lasted over twenty years, focused on a single species of harvester ant, and has been conducted on a single twenty-five-acre site, part of a cattle ranch in Arizona. This is, to say the least, a striking contrast of research styles, and one that provokes strongly conflicting reactions as to their relative value.

There is disdain in the *Nature* review of *Ants at Work* that Gordon's book is based upon 'only one of about 300 ant genera' and that 'unrepresentative' of ant behaviour. The style of Gordon's research is also subtly impugned when the reviewer comments that the inhabitants of Paradise, Arizona, have become used to her and her researchers 'crawling around' in what has 'become [their] favourite field'. This description implies an almost suburban vista, a piffling patch; even mentioning the name of the town suggests prelapsian, labour-free ease. As it happens, Paradise is *not* the nearest town to the experimental site – that position is occupied by Portal. It is all a far cry from Wilson's multiple-species collecting trips into the 'inexpressible unknown'. Gordon, perhaps, implicitly condemns Wilson along with his ants for being 'relentless' and 'fanatical'. Conversely, in Wilson's Humboldtian world, Gordon has not forged her knowledge in the necessary fires of manly exploration and self-sacrifice.

The work of Gordon and Wilson also differs in the scale and conduct of their respective projects, which might be termed single-species ecology and grand narrative. Though both have researched ant behaviour in detail, Wilson's ultimate aim has always been to produce a grand evolutionary narrative from his findings. While Gordon is interested in evolution, she is more cautious about using her research to reach over-arching or comparative zoological conclusions.[8]

When scientists, as in this case, cannot agree on what constitutes a valid style of research, no 'fact' generated by one camp can persuade its opponents, for they reject the methods by which it was decided upon, and the purpose for which it was sought.

TACIT ASPECTS OF THE DEBATE: THE NATURE OF ANTS

Just as Gordon and Wilson see the persona of the researcher differently, so it is for the ants themselves. Their differences over fixed versus flexible behaviour, random versus purposeful, are due in part to the different values of labour and society that they read into their ants.

A 1954 portrayal of the hard-working harvester ant.

Each myrmecologist has a behaviour that, for him or her, defines the condition of being an ant. For Gordon, it is working, hence the title of her book. For Wilson, it is fighting. Very little of *Ants at Work* is devoted to conflict, apart from a chapter describing how a colony manages its interactions with neighbours so as to avoid conflict during its mature phase. Wilson, on the other hand, takes weaver ants with their 'chronic border skirmishes' as his norm, claiming:

Fighting is normal behaviour for Wilson's ants. Here, in a drawing of 1994, a *Polyergus* worker attacks a *Formica fusca* worker during a slave raid.

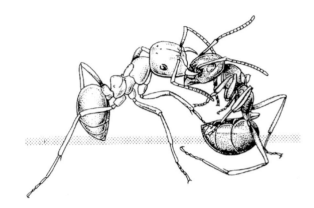

Ants . . . are arguably the most aggressive and warlike of all animals. They far exceed human beings in organized nastiness; our species is by comparison gentle and sweet-tempered. The foreign policy aim of ants can be summarized as follows: restless aggression, territorial conquest, and genocidal annihilation of neighbouring colonies wherever possible. If ants had nuclear weapons, they would probably end the world in a week.[9]

Wilson's bellicose weaver ants portrayed in 1928 by the utopian myrmecologist Forel in peacable cooperation.

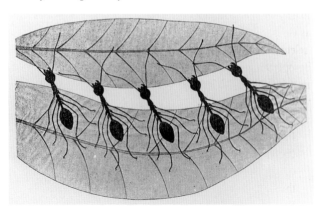

Though both researchers would qualify their descriptions with the admission that other species behave differently, the point remains that each has chosen one particular characteristic of ant as their archetype, a choice that reveals their respective paradigms of 'normal' ant behaviour. Their choices of exemplar cannot be related naïvely to their own behaviour. Wilson, far from being combative in everyday life, is renowned for his old-fashioned Southern courtesy. Even so, something in his cultural context must be invoked to explain the irresistible reading of conflict as the constant framework for his observations.

Gordon and Wilson's treatments of worker coordination are also markedly distinct, a kind of systemic autopoeia and Marxist subordination respectively. Gordon frequently emphasizes the lack of control from above. 'The basic mystery about ant colonies is that there is no management.'[10] This lack of explicit organization means there is an absence of purposefulness, or goal-directedness, from the perspective of the individual ant. Each ant is '[un]aware of what must be done to complete any colony task'. Wilson does not, of course, believe that the queen or any other ant issues orders, or that ants have any purpose in mind as they go about their business. However, Wilson's ants, as Gordon pointed out, are described as acting with a curious, 'relentless' focus. The reason for this is that Wilson seems to be operating with a final dictator, a final maker of purpose, in mind: natural selection.[11] In service of this master, Wilson writes, ants are effectively communists:

In our view, the competitive edge that led to the rise of the ants as a world-dominant group is their highly developed, self-sacrificial colonial existence. It would appear that socialism really works under some circumstances. Karl Marx just had the wrong species.[12]

Wilson's choice of guiding metaphors for his research are not difficult to explain when one considers his social conservatism, the product of living and working through the Cold War.

The origin of organization within Gordon's system, as I have already described, is not primarily from within its members' genes; instead it relies upon extrinsic factors. Of these, the most interesting to Gordon appear to be ant-ant interactions. The frequency with which an ant bumps into a colleague engaged in foraging, for example, might determine the probability of its joining in that activity itself. In short, the organization of the colony arises from within the system. Gordon is explicit about the inspiration for this way of thinking: Artificial Intelligence (AI) theory and computational systems.[13] She was part of the generation, described in the previous chapter, who enjoyed Hofstadter and similar philosophers, using their work as a springboard for their myrmecology. Gordon's confidence in engaging with other disciplines contrasts with Wilson's attitude. Since the beginning of his career he has had to fight to justify the importance of 'traditional biology' in the face of the challenge from molecular biology; James Watson, co-discoverer of the structure of DNA and one of Wilson's colleagues at Harvard, scoffed that if the university seriously wanted to promote research into evolution, it would surely be 'out of [its] mind' to hire an ecologist. Thus he has been less willing to engage with other disciplines.

Gordon mentions a very interesting assumption hidden with AI theory, so influential in her work. Its models are predicated upon the understanding that each member of the system, each node of the network, is equal, or qualitatively identical.[14] It is easy to see how this assumption has liberated Gordon to re-think the organization of the nest, and to hypothesize that workers can switch task as required. It is the opposite to

Wilson's rigid task allocation, his 'factory-workers', who are not prominently described as ever operating on a different part of the production line.[15] Wilson's vision is easily read as oligarchy, Gordon's as an affirmation of egalitarianism. This state of affairs, of course, chimes with the criticisms made of Wilson's allegedly 'sexist', 'racist' *Sociobiology* (1975), which supposedly inscribed various inequalities into nature.

Certainly, it is tempting to read these conflicting attitudes as a product of their authors' cultures: Deep South values and Harvard elitism on the one hand, and northern California idealism on the other. (Gordon herself is more inclined to trace her attitudes to the politically liberal area of New York in which she grew up.) The contrasts are also reminiscent of different generational concepts of the working world. Men of Wilson's era tended to presume they would have a career for life. Indeed, he with his 'destiny' has been an example of this, promised tenure from the outset at Harvard. Gordon's ants, available for relocation and reallocation, perhaps speak to her own understanding of the working world (more open, too, to women). Though neither myrmecologist ascribes consciousness to ants, Gordon is more inclined to talk in terms an of ant's 'experience' while Wilson tends to concentrate on the purposes of the system. This subtle difference perhaps indicates in Gordon more confidence in the (female) individual's identity in the world, a world not defined for her by superpower stand-offs, but rather a world of work. Whatever the reasons, there is little room to doubt that Gordon's biology is built upon an egalitarian system of members, while Wilson's clearly highlights caste stratification.

In a whole range of ways, therefore, *both* myrmecologists 'describe ants in a way consistent with the research programme that they [have] created'.

The film *AntZ* (1998) helps makes sense of this debate; it contextualizes its significance and provides further evidence for its tacit, cultural components outlined above. I can find no evidence that the film's makers were *au fait* with the details of the dispute then going on in myrmecology. This actually makes the case stronger, suggesting a common cultural context, a questioning of the new values of work, informing both the populist world of DreamWorks and the esoteric one of social entomology.

The story goes that Princess Bala, sick of her royal destiny, comes down to the workers' bar and meets Z, who instantly falls in love. In order to see her again, he switches places with his friend Weaver, a soldier; along with all the other soldiers Z takes part in a military parade that processes before the royals, hoping against hope that Bala might spot him in the ranks. Z's optimism is in vain; moreover, he is promptly sent into battle along with the rest of the army. The confrontation has been rigged by the evil General Mandible, who wants to kill all soldiers loyal to the queen in preparation for his coup and take-over with Bala as his (unwilling) consort. Z is the only survivor, and returns to a hero's welcome – much to Mandible's chagrin. There follows a confrontation in the royal court; Z ends up dragging Bala off and falling with her down the rubbish chute, into the outside world. Seizing his chance, he sets off with Bala in tow to find the legendary 'Insectopia' about which he has heard. Mandible sends his troops after the pair, and advances his plans to kill the worker caste by flooding the nest. Bala is captured and brought back to the nest where she discovers Mandible's plans; Z arrives soon after, having chased her. The cavern floods, but Z persuades the workers to form a

Changing places: worker Z as a soldier, soldier Weaver as a worker in *AntZ*

living tower that reaches up to the surface of the earth. All the ants are rescued, the General is defeated, and Z, of course, gets the girl.

Curiously enough, something akin to flexible task allocation is a central concern of the plot. Though the film deals with nothing so subtle as varieties of caste and behaviour among workers, it is Z and Weaver's ability to switch places – from worker to soldier and vice versa – that is the catalyst for the story. It is also a cause for much confusion and anger on the part of the other ants. Weaver's colleagues at the rock-face chide him for working too hard; Bala's mother flies off the handle because the Princess has been mixing up her life with the workers'. Perhaps the greatest outrage is that sparking the palace confrontation: the discovery that the so-called war hero is in fact a worker. Everyone in authority seems to feel personally affronted by this, and the rest of the colony threatens to revolt as a result.

More generally, the film explores the issue of individual choice. From the opening monologue to the final voiceover, the characters return to this theme over and over again. Z's desire to make his own choices is echoed by the Princess. 'Everyone has their place', her mother tells her. 'What if I don't like my place?' Bala insists. Z's attitude is reinforced when his dying friend in the termite battle tells him 'Don't make my mistake. Don't follow orders your whole life. Think for yourself.' Bala implores Mandible's ant, come to capture her in Insectopia, not to follow his orders: 'Just for once, can't you think for yourself?' And when the pair try to thwart Mandible's flood, it is hopeless trying to persuade the workers not to dig through the wall holding back the water when those were their orders. 'Stop digging!' begs Z. 'On whose authority?' the supervisor replies. 'On your own authority!' retorts the exasperated Z.

So how should DreamWorks' fable about individuality be

read? Astonishingly, at least one reviewer commented on its 'Marxist propaganda'.[16] Presumably, he was impressed by the fact that, after all those fine words about personal choice, it was a communal effort that saved the colony. During this episode, Z appears to embrace collectivism, proclaiming 'We are the colony!' Moreover, Z's Insectopia, the promised land of individuality, turns out to be nothing more than a park rubbish bin, with rotting food scattered around it. It is the kind of review one could imagine Wilson writing, reluctantly descrying socialism amongst his beloved insects. Against this interpretation must be set the film's gently derogatory attitude towards the collective masses, with their million-strong line dances and easy suasion by Mandible's rabble-rousing. When one considers these aspects of the film, a Marxist viewing seems contrary.

A more obvious way to see the film would be as an exaggeration of Gordon's position: a celebration of individualism and personal freedom. As Z jokes at the end, the movie was 'your average boy meets girl, boy likes girl, boy changes underlying social order story'. Not only was his uniqueness affirmed by finding his true love, he also up-ended the collective tyranny of the colony, practising what he preached in his numerous heartfelt speeches.

But I do not think that this is right either. Z's colony is not a straight, old-fashioned dictatorship, for all its harshness and despite the proletarian nature of many of its members. Starting with that comparison with the Dow Jones skyline, there are many clever nods to the modern world of work. For example, Z complains in the bar that he can't get interested in any of the worker females he meets: 'They're career girls . . . they're obsessed with digging.' A worker supervisor warns Weaver, when caught chatting, 'anybody who doesn't meet his quota is going to be downsized'. Best of all, when the workers psych

The colony in *AntZ* contains plenty of propaganda like this, highlighting the film's theme of work.

themselves up to start a job, they chant back and forth 'You got it!', the one-time Burger King slogan muttered reluctantly each time an employee handed something over the counter to the customer.

Thus I suggest the Cold War collectivist/individualist axis is not the correct one against which to measure the film. Rather it is a reflection on the modern experience of work, and the extent to which that provides identity. During the 1950s, '60s and '70s there was a sense that the demands of labour were shortly to decline. Increasing mechanization was confidently predicted to release humans from the need to work in the twenty-first century, leaving only the so-called 'problem of leisure' – what to do in all that spare time.[17] (It was, of course, in this period that ants inspired the birth of AI; they, or their mechanical analogues, would be our future drudges.) But with the year 2000 rapidly approaching, the inaccuracy of such visions became patently apparent. Though white-collar work in the west, at least, was not physically repressive, there was a new slavery to short-term share value. This resulted in the tyranny of management consultancy as company boards engaged in a faster than ever process of takeovers, liquidations and mergers. The individual began to change job more rapidly as companies sprang up, restructured, or vanished overnight. Perhaps because of the extra effort required to keep up with change (or because of the day-to-day inefficiencies it produced) an ever-lengthening working day was also observed in all but the poorest paid. 'I'm a soil relocation engineer' muses Z, echoing the comically inflated job-title currency that has arisen since people started needing to produce CVs every six months for their 'flexible' careers. Like Gordon's ants, humans are expected to engage in flexible task allocation, or in IBM's phrase, be 'change agents'.[18]

A paradigm for the new identity, based upon work, is modelled by the historian Nikolas Rose in his essay 'Obliged to be free'. His oxymoronic title captures well the confusing and contradictory dogma which forces individuals to construct their

Leaf-cutter ants such as these were displayed in the 'Mind Zone' of London's Millennium Dome. Like other exhibits, they were intended to inspire and motivate the modern citizen.

identities through consumer 'choice', to pay for which they remain subjected to the game of musical chairs that is the new working world. One might also point to an increased pressure to find identity in one's career: to bring attitude and cool into the workplace. The combination of these ideologies has an absurd, tacit result: that the purpose of work is to afford a designer blouse to wear to work. Thinking along these lines, Z tries to cheer himself up with the thought 'I'm insignificant – but with attitude!'[19] Another of the workers' slogans in *AntZ* suggests beautifully this designer self-management. 'Be the ball!' they cry as they form a living demolition machine. Their shout echoes a hundred recent marketing devices, such as the Calvin Klein perfume 'Be', or Nike's advice, 'Just do it'.

Z's conclusion to the film, as the camera rolls back up to the real New York skyline, drawing with it the moral from the animal to the human realm, is very unsatisfactory when one thinks about it:

> You know, I finally feel like I found my place. And you know what, it's right back where I started. But the difference is, this time I chose it.

Z has not actually changed the social structure at all. He has merely replaced General Mandible as its heir apparent. He believes that he has chosen this destiny, but we have no reason to believe that any of the other ants will get to kiss the princess. Like Rose's workers, Z has disciplined himself to accept social strictures by buying into the pretence of choice.

I suggest that Gordon and Wilson's debate is unresolved for the same reason that *AntZ* has an ambiguous interpretation. Worker flexibility *is* our current guiding norm, but we are not sure whether we like it. The future is also uncertain. Who will win this myrmecological argument, and what will be the fact of the matter in ten, twenty or fifty years' time?

Since scientists are humans, their culture conditions the types of questions they ask, the phenomena they look for, and the metaphors and models they use to describe them. In other words, no scientific debate is ever settled within a laboratory hermetically sealed from the outside world. As Bruno Latour has argued, a 'fact' is something that is decided upon at the closure of a dispute, not something that can be used to settle it. It is no easier to predict the future interpretation of ants at work than it is to anticipate our attitudes to human work. Indeed, history suggests that the outcome of the latter debate is likely to determine the resolution of the former. I have argued (Chapter 6) that the methodological and cultural dimensions attached to information theory and Artificial Intelligence have shaped recent myrmecological debates, and I think it likely that it will be decided in part by these factors, too. For one thing, the older generation of myrmecologists will eventually pass away, leaving no one to dispute with the technophiles. Moreover, there is no sign that information technology is yet stagnating. As long as there are new developments in artificial systems, there is inspiration to search these things out in the natural world – to use them to model the behaviour of ants.

The ant is culturally constructed, and I for one am intrigued by its future.

Timeline of the Ant

c. 100-200 MILLION BC

Primitive ant-wasps (*Sphecomyrma*) begin to develop social forms of life in the supercontinent Laurasia, containing present-day Europe, Asia and North America. Meanwhile in Gondwanaland, the supercontinent including Africa, South America, Australia and South Asia, other primitive ants have emerged whose little-altered descendants can still be found in Australia

c. 65 MILLION BC

All major lineages of the family Formicidae, containing the full range of modern ant forms, have developed

c. 25-40 MILLION BC

Family Formicidae has proliferated right across the globe except Antarctica

900 BC

Solomon recommends his sluggardly readers to emulate the ant

c. 1250

In his zoological treatise *De Animalibus*, Albertus Magnus adds to conventional bestiary descriptions new observations of ant behaviour

1519

The island of Hispaniola is 'tortured by a multitude of ants', which are finally rebuffed after two years through the 'divine clemency and intercession of the glorious St Saturnine', according to Gonzalo Oviedo in his *Historia general y natural de las Indias* (1535)

c. 1600

Europeans begin keeping sugar in their cupboards

c. 1734-42

René Antoine Ferchault de Réaumur writes but does not publish his book on ants, seventh and last in his series on insects

1747

William Gould writes *An Account of English Ants*

c. 1918

Fire ants of the subgenus *Solenopsis* invade the United States, arriving first in Mobile, Alabama

c. 1920

Supercolony of Argentine ants establishes itself in Europe

1935

Building on earlier guidelines, German law forbids the killing of wood ants on the grounds that they contribute to 'forest hygiene'

1954

Giant communist ants terrorize America in the film *Them!*

1963

William Hamilton proposes kin selection as a means to explain the evolutionary success of sterile worker forms of ant

1966

Discovery of *Sphecomyrma* specimen in amber, the missing link between ants and wasps, by a retired couple in New Jersey

800 BC	600 BC	440 BC	c. 380 BC	AD 350
Hesiod records that Zeus turned ants into men and women as companions for Aeacus	Aesop raises the profile of the ant in fable	Herodotus in his *History* records the presence in India of ants smaller than dogs but larger than foxes	Plato in his *Phaedon* identifies uneducated yet diligent citizens as reincarnated ants.	According to St Jerome's *Life of Malchus* (AD 391), ants inspire Malchus to return to his monastery where, as in the ants' nest, *omnium omnia sunt*

1810	1874	1890s	1905	1910
Pierre Huber writes *Recherches sur les Mœurs des Fourmis Indigènes* 'On the behaviour of native ants', having collaborated with his blind father, François Huber, in their study	Auguste Forel combines for the first time the taxonomic and behavioural study of ants in *Les Fourmis de la Suisse* ('Ants of Switzerland')	Argentine ants enter the United States aboard ships carrying coffee or sugar from Argentina, then expand throughout California and the Southern states	H. G. Wells publishes his short story 'Empire of the Ants'	William Morton Wheeler establishes myrmecology (the word itself coined *c.* 1906) as a serious scientific discipline with the publication of *Ants*. He proposes the concept of the ant colony as organism

1970s	1975	1991	1991	1998	2000
Comparisons between ant colonies and computers start to be made	E. O. Wilson makes ants famous by using their behaviour as the exemplar of his controversial sociobiology	Virtual ants and ant robots are developed to solve problems of telecommunication and space exploration	Bernard Werber publishes his cult hit *Empire of the Ants*	Woody Allen contemplates the role of the human worker in *AntZ*; Aesop's fable of the ant and the grasshopper is re-told in *A Bug's Life*	Success of Argentine ants' supercolony in California is attributed to unprecedented cooperation between genetically related nests

References

1 INTRODUCTION

1 http://home.att.net/~B-P.TRUSCIO/STRANGER.htm
2 René A. F. de Réaumur, *The Natural History of Ants*, trans. W. M. Wheeler (New York, 1926), p. 131.
3 Réaumur, *Natural History of Ants*, p. 222.
4 Edward O. Wilson, *Naturalist* (Harmondsworth, 1995), p. 287.
5 The best introduction to all things myrmecological is Bert Hölldobler and Edward O. Wilson, *Journey to the Ants: A Story of Scientific Exploration* (Cambridge, MA and London, 1994), from which this chapter draws extensively. Hölldobler and Wilson's earlier book, *The Ants* (Berlin and Heidelberg, 1990) won the Pulitzer Prize and contains just about everything one could ever wish to know about these insects.
6 Abraham Lincoln, *Collected Works of Abraham Lincoln*, ed. Roy P. Basler (New Brunswick, NJ, 1990), vol. II, p. 222.
7 Hölldobler and Wilson, *Journey to the Ants*, Preface.
8 Charlotte Sleigh, 'Brave New Worlds: Trophallaxis and the Origin of Society in the Early Twentieth Century', *Journal for the History of the Behavioral Sciences*, XXXVIII (2002), pp. 133–56.

1 Henry McCook, *Ant Communities and How They Are Governed: A Study in Natural Civics* (New York and London, 1909), p. 11.
2 Auguste Forel, *Out of my Life and Work*, trans. Bernard Miall (London, 1937), pp. 22–3.
3 *Ibid.*, p. 25.
4 E. O. Wilson, *Naturalist* (Harmondsworth, 1995), pp. 52–3.
5 *Ibid.*, p. 52.
6 José Maria Sanchez-Silva, *Ladis and the Ant*, trans. Michael Heron (London, Toronto and Sydney, 1968).
7 All Vietnamese references from Alan Farrell, 'A People Not Strong: Vietnamese Images of the Indochina War', *Vietnam Generation Journal*, IV (1992) http://lists.village.virginia.edu/sixties/HTML_docs/Texts/Narrative/Farrell_Not_Strong.html
8 McCook, *Ant Communities*, p. 53.
9 Maurice Maeterlinck, *The Life of the Ant*, trans. Bernard Miall (London, Toronto, Melbourne and Sydney, 1930), pp. 60 and 149–50.
10 Forel, *Out of my Life and Work*, pp. 21–2.
11 *Los Angeles Times*, 30 June 2002.
12 Susan Stewart, *On Longing: Narratives of the Miniature, the Gigantic, the Souvenir, the Collection* (London, 1984).
13 E. van Bruyssel, *The Population of an Old Pear-Tree; Or, Stories of Insect Life* (London, 1870), p. 17.
14 *Ibid.*, p. 50.
15 Arthur O. Lovejoy, *The Great Chain of Being: A Study in the History of an Idea* (Cambridge, MA, 1964 [1936]), p. 190.
16 Thomas Bulfinch, *The Age of Fable; Or, Stories of Gods and Heroes* (New York, 1948), chap. 12.

17 Homer, *The Iliad*, trans. E. V. Rieu (Harmondsworth, 1950), p. 298.

18 *Ibid.*, p. 299.

19 Bulfinch, *The Age of Fable*, chap. 11.

20 Aesop, *Fables of Aesop*, trans. S. A. Handford (Harmondsworth, 1964), p. 143.

21 Adele M. Fielde, *Chinese Nights' Entertainment: Forty Stories Told by Almond-Eyed Folk Actors in the Romance of the Strayed Arrow* (New York and London, 1893), pp. 18–24.

22 *Fables of Aesop*, p. 152.

23 *Ibid.*, p. 140.

24 *Ibid.*, p. 157.

25 The song was performed and recorded for an English-speaking translator in 1971 by Thomas Jangala. R.M.W. Dixon and Martin Duwell, eds, *The Honey-Ant Men's Love Song and other Aboriginal Song Poems* (Queensland, 1990), pp. 52–69.

26 Hans Heinz Ewers, *The Ant People*, trans. Clifton Harby Levy (London, 1927), p. 319.

3 ANTS AS MODELS

1 Proverbs 6: 6–8

2 La Fontaine does, however, re-use 'The Pigeon and the Ant', described in the previous chapter.

3 Jean de La Fontaine, *The Complete Tales in Verse*, trans. G. Waldman (Manchester, 2000), p. viii.

4 Quoted in Anon., *Lessons Derived from the Animal World* (London, 1851), vol. II, p. 235.

5 *Ibid.*, pp. 4–5.

6 *Ibid.*, pp. 147–8.

7 See J.F.M. Clark, '"The Complete Biography of Every

Animal": Ants, Bees, and Humanity in Nineteenth-Century England', *Studies in History and Philosophy of Biological and Biomedical Sciences*, XXIX (1998), pp. 249–67.

8 A. S. Byatt, *Angels and Insects* (London, 1995), p. 94.

9 *Ibid.*, pp. 21–2.

10 Anon., *Lessons Derived from the Animal World*, pp. 179 and 34.

11 Byatt, *Angels and Insects*, p. 74.

12 *Ibid.*, p. 38.

13 Anon., *Lessons Derived from the Animal World*, pp. 199–200.

14 *Ibid.*, p. 36.

15 *Ibid.*, p. 8.

16 Peter Kropotkin, *Mutual Aid: A Factor of Evolution* (London, 1987 [1902]), pp. 27–33 and 235–6.

17 Auguste Forel, *Out of my Life and Work*, trans. Bernard Miall (London, 1937), p. 340.

18 Auguste Forel, *The Social World of the Ants Compared With That of Man*, trans. C. K. Ogden (London 1928), vol. II, p. 351.

19 Forel, *Out of my Life and Work*, p. 332.

20 Frederick R. Prete, 'Can Women Rule the Hive? The Controversy over Honey Bee Gender Roles in British Beekeeping Texts of the Sixteenth–Eighteenth Centuries', *Journal of the History of Biology*, XXIV (1991), pp. 113–44.

21 Jean-Marc Drouin, 'L'Image des Sociétés d'Insectes en France à l'Epoque de la Révolution', *Revue de Synthèse*, IV (1992), pp. 333–45.

22 Henry McCook, *Ant Communities and How They Are Governed: A Study in Natural Civics* (New York and London, 1909), pp. 156–7.

23 Anon., *Lessons Derived from the Animal World*, p. 185.

24 E. van Bruyssel, *The Population of an Old Tree; Or, Stories of Insect Life* (London, 1870), p. 64.

25 Byatt, *Angels and Insects*, pp. 26–7 and 39.

26 Forel, *Out of My Life and Work*, pp. 188–9.

27 Hans Heinz Ewers, *The Ant People*, trans. Clifton Harby Levy (London, 1927), p. 43.

28 Ewers, *The Ant People*, pp. 23–4.

29 Sarah Jansen, 'Chemical-Warfare Techniques for Insect Control: Insect "Pests" in Germany Before and After World War I', *Endeavour*, XXIV (2000), pp. 28–33.

4 THE ENEMY WITHOUT

1 Paolo Palladino, *Entomology, Ecology and Agriculture: The Making of Scientific Careers in North America, 1885–1985* (Amsterdam, 1996); Charles E. Rosenberg, *No Other Gods: On Science and American Social Thought*, revised and expanded edn (Baltimore and London, 1997); W. Conner Sorensen, *Brethren of the Net: American Entomology, 1840–1880* (Tuscaloosa and London, 1995).

2 A similar incident (if not the same one) is described in Karen Blixen, *Out of Africa* (Harmondsworth, 1980), pp. 279–82.

3 Anon., *Lessons Derived from the Animal World* (London, 1851), vol. II, p. 205.

4 Auguste Forel, *The Social World of the Ants Compared With That of Man*, trans. C. K. Ogden (London 1928), vol. I, p. 259.

5 Henry W. Bates, *Naturalist on the River Amazons* (London, 1863), vol. II, pp. 362–3.

6 Thomas Belt, *The Naturalist in Nicaragua* (London, 1874), pp. 17–29.

7 J. Vosseler, 'Die Ostafrikanische Treiberameise', *Der Pflanzer*, I (1905), pp. 289–302.

8 William M. Mann, 'Stalking Ants, Savage and Civilised', *National Geographic Magazine*, LXVI (1934), pp. 171–92.

9 Hans Heinz Ewers, *The Ant People*, trans. Clifton Harby Levy (London, 1927), pp. vi and 77.

10 *Ibid*., pp. 80–81.

11 Quoted in Forel, *Social World of the Ants*, vol. II, pp. 186–7.

12 Auguste Forel, *The Social World of the Ants Compared With That of Man*, trans. C. K. Ogden (London 1928), vol. II, pp. 186–7.

13 *Ibid*., p. 189.

14 Arthur E. Shipley, 'Foreword', *Bulletin of Entomological Research*, I (1910), pp. 1–6.

15 H. Maxwell Lefroy, with F. M. Howlett, *Indian Insect Life: A Manual of the Insects of the Plains (Tropical India)* (Calcutta, Simla and London, 1909).

16 Patrick Parrinder, *Shadows of the Future, H.G. Wells, Science Fiction and Prophecy* (Liverpool, 1995).

17 H. G. Wells, *The Country of the Blind and Other Stories* (London, 1911), p. 499.

18 *Ibid*., p. 512.

19 Hugh Walpole, *The Dark Forest* (London, 1916), p. 124.

20 Alex Bowlby, *The Recollections of Rifleman Bowlby* (London, 1999), pp. 50–51.

21 Spike Milligan, *Rommel? Gunner Who?* (Harmondsworth, 1981), p. 61.

22 T. H. White, *The Once and Future King* (London, 1962 [1958]), p. 119.

23 *Oxford Encyclopedic English Dictionary*.

24 Christopher Hope, *Darkest England* (London, 1996), p. 3.

25 *Ibid*., p. 35.

26 *Ibid*., p. 75.

27 *Ibid*., pp. 46–7.

28 *Ibid*., p. 111.

29 Derek Walcott, *Omeros* (London, 1990), p. 31.

30 *Ibid.*, pp. 61–2.

31 *Ibid.*, pp. 128, 145–6 and 215.

32 *Ibid.*, p. 294.

33 *Ibid.*, p. 318.

34 *Ibid.*, pp. 243–6.

5 THE ENEMY WITHIN

1 Thomas Belt, *The Naturalist in Nicaragua* (London, 1911), pp. 83–4, 151 and 329–30.

2 *Ibid.*, pp. 237–8.

3 *Ibid.*, p. 158.

4 *Ibid.*, p. 166.

5 Charlotte Sleigh, 'Empire of the Ants: H. G. Wells and Tropical Entomology', *Science as Culture*, X (2001), pp. 33–71.

6 Belt, *Naturalist in Nicaragua*, p. 136.

7 A. S. Byatt, *Angels and Insects* (London, 1995), p. 38.

8 Hans Heinz Ewers, *The Ant People*, trans. Clifton Harby Levy (London: 1927), p. vii.

9 Andrew Pulver, 'Swat Team', *The Guardian*, 27 June 1998.

10 E. O. Wilson, *Naturalist* (Harmondsworth, 1996), p. 283.

11 Italo Calvino, *The Watcher and Other Stories* (San Diego, New York and London, 1971).

12 *Ibid.*, p. 151.

13 *Los Angeles Times*, Orange County edition, 6 November 1999.

14 *Los Angeles Times*, Bulldog edition, 26 September 1999.

15 Letter to *Los Angeles Times*, 29 July 2000.

16 *Los Angeles Times*, Bulldog edition, 26 September 1999.

17 *Los Angeles Times*, Orange County edition, 3 December 1999.

18 Letter to *Los Angeles Times*, 29 July 2000.

19 'Ant supercolony dominates Europe,' BBC News Science/Tech, 16 April 2002.

http://news.bbc.co.uk/hi/english/science/tech/newsid_19
32000/1932509.stm

20 Quotation supposedly taken from *Business Week* 1 June 1991. Cited at http://www.ngos.net/blockers.html The source however, appears to be spurious. That week's international edition of *Business Week* (actually 3 June 1991) did carry a cover story about Cresson's remarks, together with other items about the economic threat posed by Japanese manufacture, but did not quote her as saying anything quite so inflammatory, although *The Times* did.

21 Brigitte Schulz, 'The United States and Future Core Conflict', *Journal of World-Systems Research*, I (1995), p. 30.

22 http://goldsea.com/Features/Parisasians/parisasians8. html (no date).

23 Alan Farrell, 'A People Not Strong: Vietnamese Images of the Indochina War', *Vietnam Generation Journal*, IV (1992) available at http://lists.village.virginia.edu/sixties/HTML_docs/Texts/ Narrative/Farrell_Not_Strong.html

24 *Ibid*.

25 Quoted in: http://goldsea.com/Features/Parisasians/parisasians8.html (no date). No original source given.

6 ANTS AS MACHINES

1 See Aristotle, *Parts of Animals*, 641^{a}17–641^{b}1.10; *History of Animals*, 588^{b}1.4, 588^{a}1.24–25.

2 Julien Offray de La Mettrie, *Machine Man and Other Writings*, ed. Ann Thomson (Cambridge, 1996), pp. 37–8. La Mettrie's challenge to man's hubris was achieved through opposite means by Michel de Montaigne, who

argued that humans ought to be more humble because animals too were rational.

3 Gilles A. Bazin, *The Natural History of Bees. Containing an Account of the Production, their Œconomy, the Manner of their Making Wax and Honey, and the Best Methods for the Improvement and Preservation of them*, trans. Anon. (London, 1744), p. 6. The book is itself a loose re-working of Réaumur's volume on bees.

4 *Ibid.*, p. 169.

5 *Ibid.*, pp. 247–9.

6 *Ibid.*, pp. 274–5.

7 William M. Wheeler, 'The Ant-Colony as an Organism', *Journal of Morphology*, XXII (1911), pp. 301–25.

8 Douglas R. Hofstadter and Daniel C. Dennett, *The Mind's I: Fantasies and Reflections on Self and Soul* (Harmondsworth, 1982), p. 192.

9 Kevin Kelly, *Out of Control: The New Biology of Machines* (London, 1994), pp. 395–7.

10 http://www.ai.mit.edu/projects/ants/

11 James McLurkin, 'Using Cooperative Robots for Explosive Ordnance Disposal', http://web.mit.edu/eishih/www/courses/6.836/eod-paper.pdf

12 Julia Flynn, 'British Telecom: Notes from the Ant Colony', 23 June 1997 http://www.businessweek.com/1997/25/b353218.htm S. Steward and S. Appleby, 'Mobile Software Agents for Control of Distributed Systems Based on Principles of Social Insect Behaviour', Proceedings of ICCS, II (1994), pp. 549–53.

13 Michael J. B. Krieger, Jean-Bernard Billeter and Laurent Keller, 'Ant-Like Task Allocation and Recruitment in

Cooperative Robots', *Nature*, CDVI (2000), pp. 992–5.

14 Brian Goodwin, 'All for One ... One for All', *New Scientist*, CLVIII (1998), pp. 32–5.

7 THE AMBIGUOUS ANT

1 Ann E. Haley-Oliphant, 'Deborah Gordon: Behavioral Ecologist', in *Women Life Scientists: Past, Present and Future: Connecting Role Models to the Classroom Curriculum*, eds M. L. Matyas and A. E. Haley-Oliphant (Bethesda, MD, 1997), pp. 151–72.

2 Deborah M. Gordon, 'Look to the Ant, Thou Sluggard', *Nature*, CCCLXXII (1994), p. 292.

3 Deborah M. Gordon, 'The Organization of Work in Social Insect Colonies', *Nature*, CCCLXXX (1996), pp. 121–4.

4 Jürgen Heinze, 'Pogo-Centricity', *Nature*, CDI (1999), pp. 856–7.

5 Edward O. Wilson, 'Causes of Ecological Success: The Case of the Ants', *Journal of Animal Ecology*, LVI (1987), pp. 1–9.

6 The analysis that follows may be compared with recent research in the different approaches to primatology practised by men and women respectively. See Londa Schiebinger, *Has Feminism Changed Science?* (Cambridge, MA and London, 1999), pp. 126–44.

7 Edward O. Wilson, *Naturalist* (Harmondsworth, 1995), p. 194.

8 See the special edition of *Ecology* edited by Gordon and Pamela A. Matson; *Ecology*, LXXII (1991).

9 Bert Hölldobler and Edward O. Wilson, *Journey to the Ants: A Story of Scientific Exploration* (Cambridge, MA and London, 1994), p. 59. The 'typical' male ant, they moreover claim, is a 'sperm-bearing missile'. *Ibid.*, p. 36.

10 Deborah M. Gordon, *Ants at Work: How an Insect Society is Organized* (New York, 1999), p. vii.

11 Compare against Beer's discussion of Darwin's personification of natural selection. Gillian Beer, *Darwin's Plots: Evolutionary Narrative in Darwin, George Eliot and Nineteenth-Century Fiction* (London, Boston, and Melbourne, 1985).

12 Hölldobler and Wilson, *Journey to the Ants*, p. 9.

13 Gordon, 'The Organization of Work in Social Insect Colonies', p. 122.

14 *Ibid.*, p. 122.

15 Hölldobler and Wilson call ants 'factory workers' in *Journey to the Ants*, p. 10.

16 Terry Richards, 'Film Reviews: AntZ', *Film Review* (December 1998), p. 19.

17 See, for example, E. P. Thompson, 'Time, Work-Discipline, and Industrial Capitalism', *Past and Present*, XXXVIII (1967), pp. 56–97.

18 Naomi Klein, *No Logo* (London, 2000), p. 71.

19 J. G. Ballard suggests a shocking conclusion to these trends in his novel *Super-Cannes*, based on the premise that 'work is the ultimate play' of the near future. J. G. Ballard, *Super-Cannes* (London, 2000), p. 94.

Bibliography

Aesop, *Fables of Aesop*, trans. S. A. Handford (Harmondsworth, 1964)

Bolton, Barry, *Identification Guide to the Ant Genera of the World* (Cambridge, MA, 1994)

——, *A New General Catalogue of Ants of the World* (Cambridge, MA, 1995)

Bourke, Andrew F. G. and Nigel Franks, *Social Evolution in Ants* (Princeton, 1995)

Byatt, A. S., *Angels and Insects* (London, 1995)

Chauvin, Rémy, *The World of Ants: A Science-Fiction Universe*, trans. George Ordish (London 1970)

Fabre, J. H., *Souvenirs Entomologiques: Etudes sur L'Instinct et les Mœurs des Insectes* (Paris, 1879–1907)

Forel, Auguste, *The Social World of the Ants Compared With That of Man*, trans. C. K. Ogden (London 1928)

Gordon, Deborah M., *Ants at Work: How an Insect Society is Organized* (New York, 1999)

Gotwald, William H. Jr., *Army Ants: The Biology of Social Predation* (Ithaca and London, 1995)

Gould, William, *An Account of English Ants* (London 1747)

Hölldobler, Bert, and Edward O. Wilson, *The Ants* (Berlin and Heidelberg, 1990)

—, *Journey to the Ants: A Story of Scientific Exploration*
(Cambridge, MA and London, 1994)
Huber, Pierre, *Recherches sur les Mœurs des Fourmis Indigènes*
(Paris, 1810)
Huxley, Camilla R., and David F. Cutler, *Ant-Plant Interactions*
(Oxford, 1991)
Johnson, Steven, *Emergence: The Connected Lives of Ants, Brains,
Cities and Software* (London, 2001)
Lubbock, John, *Ants, Bees and Wasps: A Record of Observations
on the Habits of the Social Hymenoptera* (London, 1882)
Maeterlinck, Maurice, *The Life of the Ant*, trans. Bernard Miall
(London, Toronto, Melbourne and Sydney, 1930)
Réaumur, René Antoine Ferchault de, *Mémoires pour Servir à
l'Histoire des Insectes, Tome Septième, Histoire des Fourmis*
(Paris, 1928; based on unpublished manuscripts c.
1734–1742)
Sorensen, W. Conner, *Brethren of the Net: American Entomology,
1840–1880* (Tuscaloosa and London, 1995)
Stewart, Susan, *On Longing: Narratives of the Miniature, the
Gigantic, the Souvenir, the Collection* (London, 1984)
Taber, Stephen Welton, *Fire Ants* (College Station, TX, 2000)
Vander Meer, Robert K., Klaus Jaffe and Aragua Cedeno, eds,
Applied Myrmecology: A World Perspective (Boulder, CO, 1990)
Werber, Bernard, *Empire of the Ants*, trans. Margaret Roques
(London, 1991)
Wheeler, W. M., *Ants: Their Structure, Development and Behavior*
(New York, 1910)
—, 'The Ant-Colony as an Organism', *Journal of Morphology*,
XXII (1911), pp. 301–25
White, T. H., *The Once and Future King* (London, 1963)
Wilson, Edward O., *Naturalist* (Harmondsworth, 1996)

Associations

INTERNATIONAL SOCIETY OF HYMENOPTERISTS

The ISH covers all aspects of original research on the
Hymenoptera (ants, bees, sawflies, wasps), including biology,
behaviour, ecology, systematics, taxonomy, genetics and
morphology. It publishes the specialist *Journal of Hymenoptera
Research*. More details of the Society can be found at:
http://iris.biosci.ohio-state.edu/ish/

INTERNATIONAL UNION FOR THE STUDY OF SOCIAL INSECTS

The IUSSI was formed to facilitate communication among
social insect researchers worldwide. It publishes the specialist
journal *Insectes Sociaux* and more details of the Union are
available at:
http://www.iussi.org/

SOCIAL INSECTS SPECIALISTS GROUP

The mission of SISG is to disseminate information on social
insects relevant to conservation. More details of the Group
can be found at:
http://research.amnh.org/entomology/social_insects/sisg.html

Websites

There are many sites devoted to ants, from the thorough to the frivolous.

Formis, a master bibliography of ant literature is available at:
http://cmave.usda.ufl.edu/~formis/

The *Social Insects World Wide Web* is more engaging than Formis for the non-specialist, and can be found at:
http://research.amnh.org/entomology/social_insects/

Myrmecology: The Scientific Study of Ants provides a good starting point to find out the basics about ant life, with suggestions on where to go next:
http://www.myrmecology.org/javaindex.htm

The website of the Ant Colony Developers Association is particularly strong on do-it-yourself advice about keeping ant farms: http://www.antcolony.org/

Ant trivia of all kinds resides at the *Ant Farm's Reading Room*:
http://alpha.zimage.com/~ant/antfarm/read/read.html

Acknowledgements

I would like to thank the friends and colleagues who have helped in the writing of this book, whether by reading drafts or contributing nuggets of ant lore: Janet Browne, Jonathan Burt, Roger Cardinal, Mark Connelly, Marion Copeland, Matthew Copping, Alex Dolby, Rod Edmond, Angela Faunch, Nick Jardine, Abigail Lustig, Dave Reason, Jonathan Sheehan, Jonathan Sleigh, Ben Thomas and Nick Thurston.

Illustrations for *Ant* were collected and reproduced thanks to a generous grant from The British Academy and the unfailingly patient and cheerful assistance of Spencer Scott at the University of Kent photographic unit.

Photo Acknowledgements

The author and publishers wish to express their thanks to the below sources of illustrative material and/or permission to reproduce it. (Some printed sources uncredited in the captions for reasons of brevity are also given below.)

Photo © ADAGP, Paris and DACS, London 2003: p. 46; photo James L. Amos, Peter Arnold Inc./Science Photo Library: p. 176; photos by the author: pp. 16, 117 (left); illustration from Thomas Belt, *The Naturalist in Nicaragua* (1911 edition): p. 118; illustrations for Thomas Bulfinch, *The Age of Fable*: pp. 46 (1942 edition) and 48 (1898 edition); photo Oscar Burriel/Science Photo Library: p. 74; photos Canterbury Cathedral Library, reproduced with kind permission of the Dean and Chapter: pp. 60 (foot), 63; photos Julie Cook/© Zoological Society of London: pp. 13, 44, 70, 89; © 2003 Cordon Art B. V. - Baarn - Holland. All rights reserved: pp. 154 (M. C. Escher woodcut *Moebius Strip II (Red Ant)*, 1963), 155 (M. C. Escher lithograph *Ant*, 1943); photo by kind permission of the Master and Fellows of Corpus Christi College, Cambridge, © Corpus Christi College, Cambridge (Ms 53, f. 198r): p. 59; illustrations from John Crompton, *Ways of the Ant* (1954) used by kind permission of the Welbourn Literary Agency: pp. 92, 179; illustration from R. Dodsley, *Select Fables of Aesop* (1800): p. 49; illustration from

J. H. Fabre, *Social Life in the Insect World* (1912): p. 61; illustrations from Auguste Forel, *Le Monde Social des Fourmis* (1921-2): p. 78, and *Social World of the Ants Compared with That of Man* (1928): pp. 31, 93, 180 (foot); drawing © Turid Forsyth: p. 180 (top); photos Pascal Goetgheluck/Science Photo Library: p. 27; illustration by kind permission of Lucas Haley: p. 150; photo © Bert Hölldobler (SEM by Ed Seling): p. 11 (top); originally published in Bert Hölldobler and Edward O. Wilson, *Journey to the Ants: A Story of Scientific Exploration*, 1994): pp. 11 (top), 180 (top); photos by kind permission of Laurent Keller: p. 161; photo (1999) by Irfan Khan, © 2003, *Los Angeles Times*, reprinted by permission: p. 134; photo James King-Holmes/Science Photo Library: p. 163; illustrations from Jean de La Fontaine's *Fables*: pp. 60 (top) (1864 edition) and 60 (foot) (1745 edition); illustrations from the anonymous *Lessons Derived from the Animal World* (1851): pp. 37, 38 (top); illustration by permission of the *Macon* (Georgia) *Telegraph and News*: p. 29; photos Peter Menzel/Science Photo Library: p. 52, 129; Museum Meermanno-Westreenianum, Den Haag (Ms. no. MMW, 10 B 25, fol. 25r): p. 6; photos © The Natural History Museum, London: pp. 24, 128, 189; photos Claude Nuridsany & Marie Perennou/Science Photo Library: pp. 21, 177; illustration from John Ogilby, *The Fables of Aesop Paraphras'd in Verse* (1665): p. 63; photo Dr Morley Read/Science Photo Library: p. 94; illustration (2002) by Al Schaben, a detail of 'Fire Ants on a Thomas Guide map', © 2003, *Los Angeles Times*, reprinted by permission: p. 133; illustration from David Sharp, *Insects* (1899): p. 100; photos Science Photo Library: p. 132, 145, 170 (left); illustrations from The Social Insects World Wide Web <http://research.amnh.org/entomology/social_insects/> by kind permission of Donat Agosti: pp. 10, 19, 53, 91; photo Stanford News Service, courtesy of Deborah Gordon: p. 170 (right); photo Volker

Index